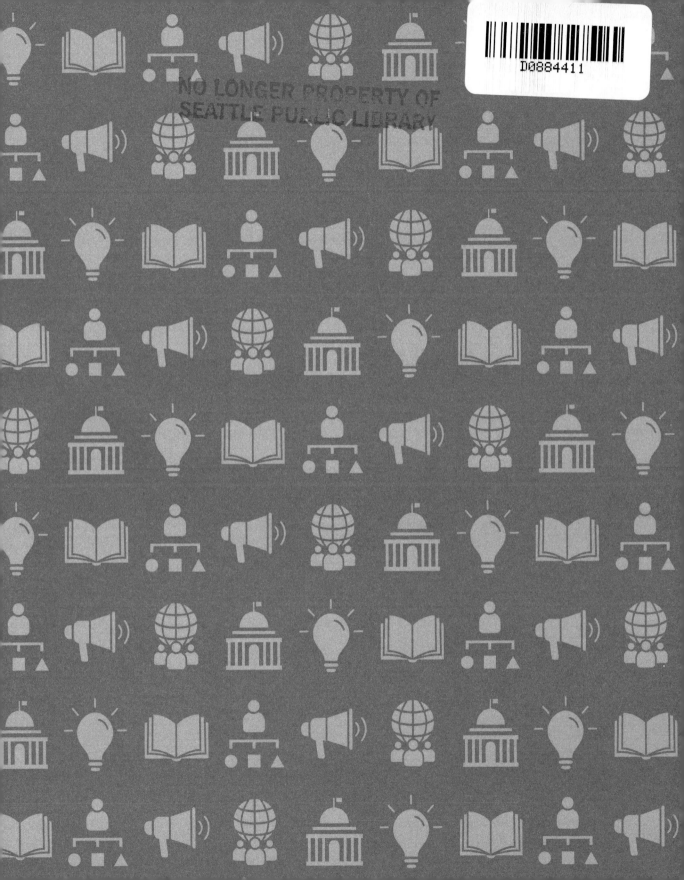

HOW POLITICS WORKS

HOW POLITICS WORKS

The CONCEPTS visually explained

Senior Editor Alison Sturgeon
Senior Art Editor Gadi Farfour
Project Editor Daniel Byrne
Editors Kathryn Hill, Andrew Humphreys,
Joanna Micklem, Victoria Pyke, Andrew Szudek
Designer Daksheeta Pattni
Illustrators Phil Gamble,
Vanessa Hamilton, Mark Lloyd
Managing Editor Gareth Jones
Managing Art Editor Lee Griffiths
Senior Production Editor Andy Hillard
Senior Production Controller Rachel Ng
Jacket Designer Vidushi Chaudhry
Senior DTP Designer Harish Aggarwal
Senior Jackets Coordinator Priyanka Sharma Saddi
Jacket Design Development Manager Sophia MTT
Publisher Liz Wheeler
Publishing Director Jonathan Metcalf
Art Director Karen Self

First American Edition, 2022
Published in the United States by DK Publishing
1450 Broadway, Suite 801, New York, NY 10018

Copyright © 2022 Dorling Kindersley Limited
DK, a Division of Penguin Random House LLC
22 23 24 25 26   10 9 8 7 6 5 4 3 2 1
001–325055–Jun/2022

A catalog record for this book is available from the Library of Congress.
ISBN 978-0-7440-5630-3

DK books are available at special discounts when purchased in bulk for sales
promotions, premiums, fund-raising, or educational use. For details, contact:
DK Publishing Special Markets,
1450 Broadway, Suite 801, New York, NY 10018
SpecialSales@dk.com

Printed and bound in UAE

For the curious
www.dk.com

MIX
Paper from
responsible sources
FSC™ C018179

This book was made with Forest Stewardship
Council ™ certified paper - one small step
in DK's commitment to a sustainable future.
For more information go to
www.dk.com/our-green-pledge

CONTENTS

ORGANIZING GOVERNMENT

POLITICAL CHANGE

CONTRIBUTORS

Paul Kelly (Consultant editor)

Paul Kelly is professor of political theory at the London School of Economics and Political Science and former pro-director. He is the author, editor, and co-editor of 17 books on contemporary political philosophy, international political theory, and British politics and ideas.

Philip Baselice (Consultant editor)

Philip Baselice teaches history at the Nysmith School and was previously professor of history at Northern Virginia Community College. He has served as a consultant on six books on history and politics. His research interests include American history, 19th- and 20th-century European history, nationalism, and decolonization.

Niheer Dasandi

Niheer Dasandi is associate professor in politics and development at the University of Birmingham. His research looks at the politics of sustainable development and human rights and has been published in leading academic journals. He is also the author of the book *Is Democracy Failing?*

Elizabeth Dowsett

Elizabeth Dowsett is a writer and editor who has contributed to many books, including DK's *Politics Is...*. Previously, she worked in the Cabinet Office of the UK Government, in other civil service departments, and in the Houses of Parliament as the political administrator for the *Guardian* newspaper.

INTERNATIONAL RELATIONS

GOVERNMENTS AROUND THE WORLD

Ann Kramer

A historian and nonfiction writer, Ann Kramer studied feminism and women's history at Sussex University. She has written or contributed to an extensive range of books on politics, feminism, and human rights. Recently, she contributed to DK's *Politics Is…* and *The Feminism Book*.

Anca Pusca

Anca Pusca is executive editor in international relations at Palgrave Macmillan, an imprint of Springer Nature. She received her PhD in international relations from the American University, School of International Studies. She is a visiting professor at the CUNY Graduate Center and the New School in New York.

Andrew Szudek

Andrew Szudek is a writer and editor who studied philosophy at Cambridge University, where he focused on political philosophy and ethics. He has worked on numerous nonfiction titles, ranging from travel guides to military history.

Marcus Weeks

Marcus Weeks has written and contributed to numerous books on politics, philosophy, psychology and the arts, including several titles in DK's "Big Ideas" series. He was the consultant editor and a contributor for DK's *How Philosophy Works*.

INTRODUCTION

Human beings have always lived in communities, and, to that extent, politics has always been with us. It is primarily a social activity—one that is concerned with how societies are organized and how they might be changed for the better. However, it is also a theoretical discipline—one that tries to answer questions such as: How is political authority justified? How much power should a government have over its citizens? What rights do citizens have, and how should they be protected?

The answers to these questions have always been disputed, and they can be grouped together into what are known as "ideologies." An ideology is a tradition of thought, and it may favor autocracy (absolute rule by one person), or democracy (rule by the people), or something in between, such as an elected monarchy. What distinguishes these ideologies from one another is that each offers a fundamentally different view of human nature. For example, defenders of autocracy, or of extensive government powers, tend to view humans as being inherently violent and in need of state control. On the other hand, defenders of democracy, or of limited government powers, tend to view humans as being inherently reasonable and capable of controlling their own destinies.

How Politics Works provides an overview of the main political ideologies and examines the range of institutions that governments use to implement their policies. Just as there are different kinds of authoritarian regimes, there are different kinds of democracies, all of which are analyzed in this book. Chapters 1 to 5 look at political theory, how governments are organized, and some of the problems governments face—such as how they should interact with each other internationally and how they should manage resources at home. Chapter 6 offers an overview of the main governments of the world today and has a look at what makes each of them unique.

FOUNDATIONS OF POLITICAL THOUGHT

The need for politics

Humans are social animals and have evolved with the natural tendency to live in social units. In order to operate successfully, these units—or societies—have had to develop ways to organize and regulate themselves for the benefit and security of their members. As a result, various forms of government have emerged. The process of establishing these distinct systems and deciding how they should operate is the business of politics.

Rulers and citizens

Throughout history, the government of society was determined by a ruler, or ruling class, and ordinary citizens had no say in the matter. Then, during the Enlightenment of the 17th and 18th centuries (see p.17), philosophers began to consider the relationship between government and those being governed and to suggest ways in which citizens could be involved in selecting their rulers.

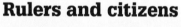

Thomas Hobbes (1588–1679)
English philosopher Thomas Hobbes felt that without authority, society would fall into anarchy. He argued that people should submit to a sovereign ruler with absolute power.

GROWTH OF CIVILIZATIONS

Since prehistoric times, humans have banded together. Early family groups of nomadic hunter-gatherers merged into clans and tribes. Later, the adoption of agricultural practices necessitated permanent settlements. These grew in size and sophistication from encampments and villages to towns and cities and extended their influence into surrounding territories, either to ally with or conquer other cities. The world's great ancient civilizations emerged from these so-called city-states, as they increased their power to become kingdoms or even empires, and the precursors of modern states. As these societies evolved, they developed varying forms of political organization, coming up with different notions of how to rule and govern the populace.

> "The administration of justice… is the principle of order in political society."
>
> Aristotle, Greek Philosopher, *Politics*, Book I (4th century BCE)

John Locke (1632–1704)
English philosopher John Locke believed society should transfer some of its rights to the government in order to ensure the people's right to their life, liberty, health, and possessions.

Jean-Jacques Rousseau (1712–78)
Swiss-born philosopher Rousseau argued that all the existing forms of government were based on inequality. He said that the power to make laws should be in the hands of the people.

The ruler is sovereign

In his book *Leviathan*, a key work of political philosophy written in 1651, Thomas Hobbes presented his argument that a powerful ruler is necessary in order to control conflict in civil society.

Anarchy and unrest

Thomas Hobbes wrote *Leviathan* during the English Civil War (1642–51), an event that strongly influenced his political philosophy. His experience of the conflict left him with a pessimistic view of human existence: life for most people, he said, was "solitary, poor, nasty, brutish, and short." He believed the war arose from disagreements in the philosophical foundations of political knowledge. He devised his own reformed theory of how people might be best governed in order to bring an end to divisiveness and also to end the conditions of war.

Without regulation of some sort, Hobbes reasoned, it would be every person for themselves in a fight for survival. This scenario, the philosopher believed, would result in a constant state of chaos, just as in the Civil War.

Hobbes believed that political authority existed in order to avoid such disorder. In return for citizens sacrificing some of their liberties, their rulers would protect them from attacks by others.

A greater good

Hobbes explained the concessions made by each individual in favor of society as a whole as a form of agreement—or "social contract," as it later became known. In forming such a contract, society itself is made into a sovereign authority, to which the individuals surrender their own authority.

In order to prevent society from descending into anarchy, Hobbes argued that this sovereign authority must be strongly enforced—and the job of enforcement is granted to the sovereign ruler. The ruler is given absolute power, taking control of all civilian, military, and judicial matters. In return, it is the sovereign's duty to ensure the protection and well-being of the population.

THE PHILOSOPHY OF THOMAS HOBBES

Hobbes was a materialist, meaning he believed that everything in the universe is physical. He therefore denied the existence of immaterial substances. As an extension of his materialism, Hobbes argued that the universe and everything in it behaves in a mechanistic way, according to scientific laws, and as a result, he rejected the idea that humans have free will. He also believed that people are, by nature, motivated by self-interest in order to satisfy their physical needs. Hobbes was the first of the philosophers to promote the idea of the social contract (see opposite).

Conflicts of interest

In any social group, there will inevitably be conflicts of interest and disputes over resources and ownership. The function of civil society is to prevent and resolve these conflicts, and to do so requires some form of government.

THE STATE OF NATURE

Without the constraints of civil society, Hobbes argued, peoples' natural state or "state of nature" would be one of constant conflict for supremacy and survival.

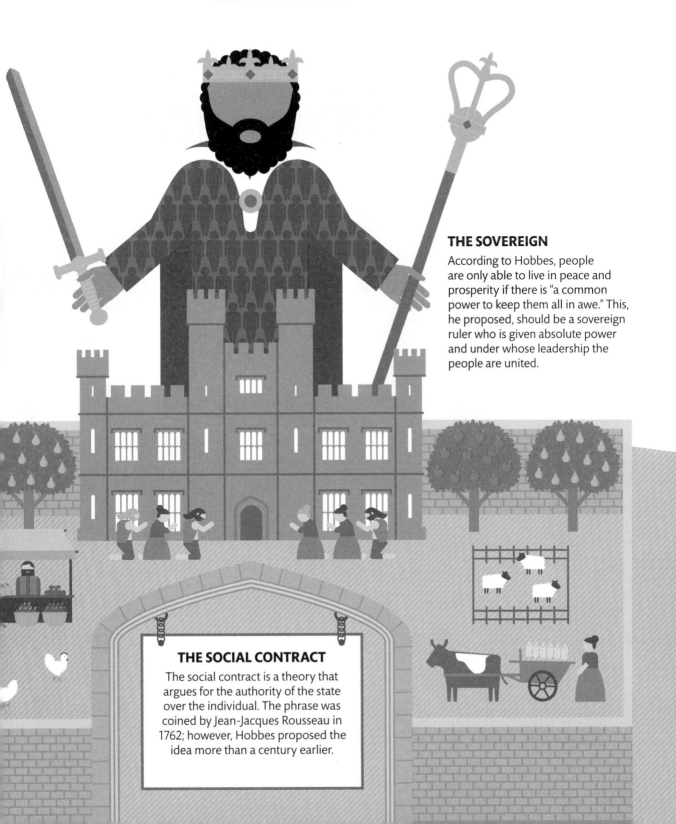

THE SOVEREIGN

According to Hobbes, people are only able to live in peace and prosperity if there is "a common power to keep them all in awe." This, he proposed, should be a sovereign ruler who is given absolute power and under whose leadership the people are united.

THE SOCIAL CONTRACT

The social contract is a theory that argues for the authority of the state over the individual. The phrase was coined by Jean-Jacques Rousseau in 1762; however, Hobbes proposed the idea more than a century earlier.

Sovereignty by consent

An influential supporter of the core Enlightenment values of liberty, equality, and rational thought, John Locke advocated for a society based on a social contract that protects the "natural rights" of its members.

The people's rights

John Locke held a more favorable opinion of human nature than Thomas Hobbes, believing that people are essentially cooperative, altruistic, and, above all, rational. Locke acknowledged that people would also want to protect their own interests and explained that each individual has a "natural right" to defend their life, health, liberty, and possessions. He further recognized that this could lead to conflicts of interest but proposed an alternative way to resolve these.

Whereas Hobbes had advocated for a strong sovereign authority to prevent conflict, Locke favored a more benign form of rulership. He argued that a successful civil society required the people to grant a government authority to rule over them. This would ensure that the government in turn protects, rather than restricts, its people's rights and freedoms. Locke believed that the core function of such a government is to secure justice by acting as an arbiter in any disputes and to respect the natural rights of

Government by consent

Both Hobbes and Locke identified that the formation of a civil society is dependent on a form of social contract, in which the people agree to give power to the government in return for their security. Locke, however, stressed the element of consent necessary in such an agreement. The people, he argued, willingly submit to the rule of a government that will protect their rights and administer justice in disputes over conflicts of interest.

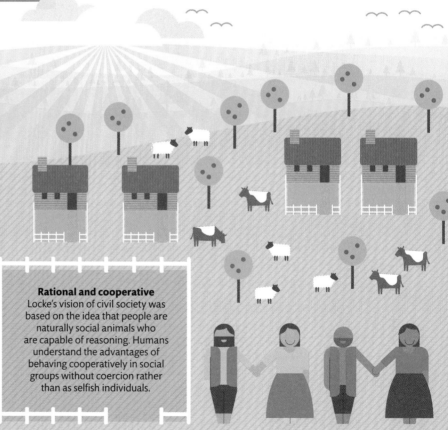

Rational and cooperative
Locke's vision of civil society was based on the idea that people are naturally social animals who are capable of reasoning. Humans understand the advantages of behaving cooperatively in social groups without coercion rather than as selfish individuals.

each citizen. He argued that if any government failed to do this, the people could overthrow it, replacing it with one that serves their interests.

Enduring influence

In Locke's opinion, as people are both rational and cooperative, they would consent to the government exerting authority over them to secure their natural rights. This interpretation of the social contract, as well as Locke's concept of an individual's rights, influenced liberal thinkers in 18th-century Europe. It had an impact in the US too: Locke's theory of rights is the source of the right to "Life, Liberty and the pursuit of Happiness," as cited in the US Declaration of Independence.

> "The **end of law is not to abolish** or restrain, **but to** preserve **and** enlarge freedom."
>
> John Locke, *Second Treatise of Civil Government* (1690)

THE ENLIGHTENMENT

During the 17th and 18th centuries, an intellectual movement known as the Enlightenment took hold of European society. Scientists and philosophers emphasized the importance of rational thought and science over faith and religion, challenging the authority of both the Church and the monarchy. The Enlightenment forced people to reexamine the way that society was organized and governed and prompted a political movement centered on the ideals of liberty, equality, and the rights of citizens that culminated in the American and French Revolutions.

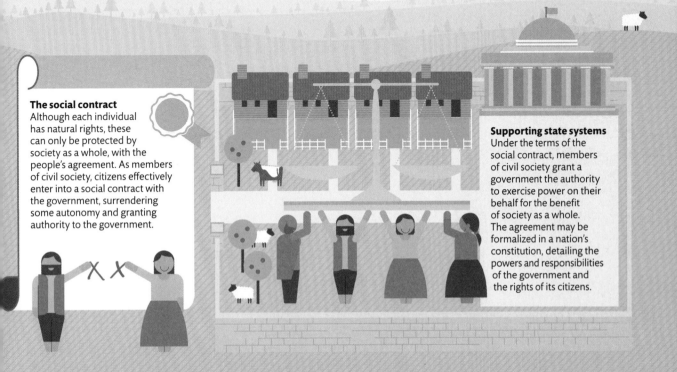

The social contract
Although each individual has natural rights, these can only be protected by society as a whole, with the people's agreement. As members of civil society, citizens effectively enter into a social contract with the government, surrendering some autonomy and granting authority to the government.

Supporting state systems
Under the terms of the social contract, members of civil society grant a government the authority to exercise power on their behalf for the benefit of society as a whole. The agreement may be formalized in a nation's constitution, detailing the powers and responsibilities of the government and the rights of its citizens.

The people are sovereign

Jean-Jacques Rousseau criticized the concept of civil society, claiming it corrupts humanity's innate goodness and restricts freedom. Instead, he advocated for a society governed by the "general will" of the people.

Society corrupts

Rousseau coined the term "the social contract" when he used it as the title of his influential political treatise, published in 1762. But his vision of how this would work in an ideal society was fundamentally different from the concept formerly envisaged by Hobbes or even Locke.

Rousseau argued that in a state of nature, humans are essentially good as well as free: because natural resources are available to all, there are no conflicts of interest. As he explained, "the fruits of the earth belong to all, but the earth itself belongs to nobody."

What spoils this ideal situation, according to Rousseau, is when a person claims a territory as their own, denying others access to its resources. In the past, civil society had protected the rights of the individual, especially the right to private property. In doing so, it created inequality and restricted freedom, fostering conflict and a corruption of people's natural goodness. Conflicts of interest were then inevitable between those who had and those who had not.

Power to the people

Rousseau's solution was a radically different form of society and the social contract: instead of people granting a government authority, as Locke had proposed, society

The "general will"

In Rousseau's ideal society, the focus is on the collective interest of the citizens, as opposed to the rights of the individual. Government should be a collective process, with people engaging directly in democracy (see pp.30–31) rather than through representatives.

Private property creates inequality

Claiming ownership of private property leads to unfair distribution of resources, and a government that protects the right to property restricts natural freedom.

should instead be governed by the people themselves. Rousseau argued that decisions should be made by consensus, expressing the "general will" of the people. This would ensure that a government preserves the interests of society as a whole—rather than just protecting individual rights—therefore restoring the natural freedom of the people.

ROUSSEAU AND THE FRENCH REVOLUTION

Just as Locke's theory of rights inspired the ideals of the American Revolution (1775–83), Rousseau provided similar inspiration in France. The French Revolution (1789–99) shared the same aspirations for the rights of citizens as the newly established American Republic, but it was Rousseau's ideas of freedom and equality, and of overthrowing the corrupt old order, that fired up the revolutionaries. Their rallying cry of "Liberté, égalité, fraternité," later adopted as a motto of the French Republic, was a direct paraphrase of the ideas set out in Rousseau's *The Social Contract*.

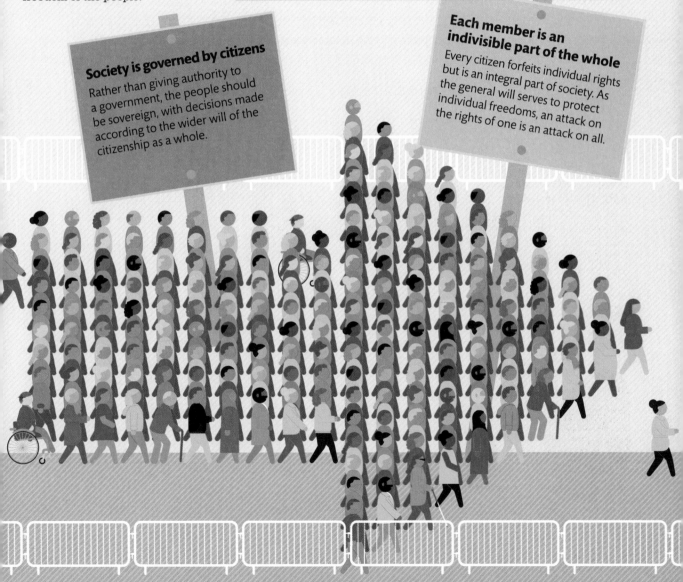

Society is governed by citizens

Rather than giving authority to a government, the people should be sovereign, with decisions made according to the wider will of the citizenship as a whole.

Each member is an indivisible part of the whole

Every citizen forfeits individual rights but is an integral part of society. As the general will serves to protect individual freedoms, an attack on the rights of one is an attack on all.

Who should rule?

Different models for ruling over a population have evolved over time, along with ideas about how best to serve the interests of those being governed. Old models of leadership by a single ruler, who most likely inherited power, supported by a privileged caste, have largely been replaced by systems that are increasingly democratic. In the modern world, most countries favor governments that are elected by the people to represent the views and aspirations of the people.

Types of leader

Government leaders reflect the different political systems of the societies they represent as well as that society's values and priorities. The selection process for leaders varies between societies: leaders may be given power out of respect, some are born to power, some seize power, and others are appointed or elected.

Tribal

Smaller tribal societies are structured like traditional families. Tribal leaders are the head of the family, providing security and protection. They are often chosen for their seniority, wisdom, and experience.

Military

Military leaders may attain power because of their skill in battle or their seniority in rank. In the past, they may have seized power through conquest; these days, it is more likely to be as a result of a coup d'etat.

1. What power have you got?
2. Where did you get it from?
3. In whose interests do you exercise it?
4. To whom are you accountable?
5. How do we get rid of you?

Tony Benn, British politician, in his last speech at the House of Commons (2001)

WHY DO WE NEED LEADERS?

Humans are by nature inclined to want to be led. Even in democracies in which people are "equal," leaders still emerge. Some are no more than figureheads, but often a single person is selected to take final responsibility for the actions of the government. Only a few political systems, such as anarchism, do not regard leaders as a necessity.

Hereditary

Historically, many nations have been ruled by monarchs—kings, queens, emperors, sultans, emirs—who were believed to have inherited a divine right to rule, which they passed to their heirs.

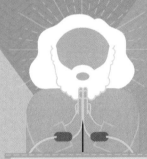

Religious

In strictly religious societies, the laws and government are thought to be divinely determined and are controlled by priests or officials of the main religion. Leaders are chosen for their moral authority and religious knowledge.

Elected

In the modern era, the ancient idea of democratic rule has come to dominate. Leaders can be directly elected by the people or by elected representatives. It is rule by the people rather than by an individual.

Wise leaders

Throughout history, some rulers have inherited their power or seized it by force, while others have been chosen for their leadership qualities, especially the traditional values of wisdom and experience.

A ruling class

It may seem obvious that one of the qualities of a good ruler is wisdom, but it was the Athenian philosopher Plato (5th century BCE) who identified the specific kind of wisdom he believed necessary in a leader. In his book *Republic*, Plato described what he considered to be an ideal society and how it should best be governed.

Plato saw society as consisting of three classes of people: the ordinary working people, the armed forces, and the educated elite. He had experienced rule by "ordinary people" in the form of Athenian democracy, under which his friend and mentor Socrates was accused of corrupting the city's youth with his ideas and sentenced to death. From this, Plato concluded that it was the educated and wise who were best suited to rule because they would be guided by reason rather than self-interest.

Philosopher kings

In Plato's ideal society, people are able to live the "good life": they are safe, happy, and behave in a moral way. It is the responsibility of rulers to create a society in which citizens can enjoy this "good life." However, said Plato, it is only philosophers who truly understand the meaning of ideals such as "good" and "right," and, as such, they are the only people capable of leading society.

He therefore advocated for a society ruled by a small, elite class of "philosopher kings." This could be brought about either by putting philosophers into positions of power or by educating rulers in the

MARCUS AURELIUS

Although he inherited rather than earned the position, Marcus Aurelius (121–180 CE) became one of the most successful and well liked of the Roman emperors. Apparently confirming Plato's advocacy of philosopher kings, Marcus Aurelius was not only an outstanding political and military leader who maintained peace and prosperity throughout his reign but also a respected philosopher. His *Meditations*, written while he was emperor, constitutes a lengthy discourse on self-improvement, personal virtue, and ethics. The work remains an inspiration to philosophers and political leaders today.

The ship of state

In Plato's *Republic*, the character Socrates likens society to a ship whose owner (the citizens) has little knowledge of seafaring. To manage the vessel, he relies on a crew of sailors (the politicians), who boast of their seafaring abilities but nevertheless need the services of a navigator (a philosopher) to determine a safe and efficient course.

The navigator
Representing the philosopher king, the navigator is the only one with the knowledge and understanding of the stars and sea necessary to set the ship's course.

discipline of philosophy. Although Plato's idea seems at odds with both traditional ideas of monarchy and modern notions of democracy, it still has influence today; in many countries, there has emerged a class of political leaders who have studied political philosophy before embarking upon their careers.

"**Until philosophers are kings... cities will never have rest from their evils.**"

Plato, *Republic* (c.375 BCE)

The ship owner
Standing for the citizens, the ship owner is nominally in charge but reliant on the navigator and the crew to reach his destination.

The crew
Often arguing among themselves, the crew (the politicians) can manage the ship but are lost without the guidance of the navigator.

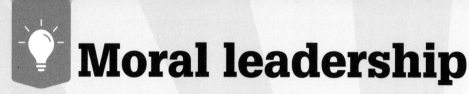

Moral leadership

Early political philosophers believed that the main role of politics was to create a society of moral citizens. The leader of such a society should therefore be a model of ethical behavior.

The virtuous ruler

A major purpose of civil society is to protect its citizens and allow them to live safe and happy lives. This is achieved by the rule of law, based on accepted moral principles of what is right and wrong and good and bad behavior. In his *Republic*, Plato argued that society should be overseen by wise philosopher kings who have the necessary knowledge to guide citizens on the true course to a happy existence (see pp.22–23).

Other political philosophies maintained that wisdom in itself is not enough. A good leader should rule in the best interests of the people and should also be seen to be just and inspire the people's respect. In short, to establish a virtuous society, a ruler must be seen to be virtuous. Even today, leaders are expected to live according to the moral standards of society and may lose the respect of the people if they fall short of these.

Leading by example

Kong Fuzi (Confucius) advocated for the concepts of *ren* and *li*. *Ren* is the understanding of how to behave in all situations, based on an individual's place in the hierarchy. *Li* means "ritual" and refers to the veneration of ancestors. To help spread the example set by the virtuous ruler, Kong Fuzi also advocated for ceremonies that emphasized these moral codes. Here, the ruler's virtues are likened to the seeds on a grass stalk, which the wind disperses in the field; there they take root and give rise to more stalks and seeds, all similarly virtuous, like the ruler.

1. The virtues of the ruler
The ruler's virtues need to be conspicuously displayed at all times to provide a positive role model for their subjects to follow.

"When we see men of worth, we should think of equaling them."
Confucius, *The Analects* (5th century BCE)

The "superior person"

Ideas about the importance of morality in the structure of society also developed in ancient China. The philosopher Kong Fuzi (551–479 BCE), known in the West as Confucius, argued that a leader should above all set an example of correct behavior for the people to follow. He proposed a hierarchical organization of society, with each member recognizing their place and showing respect for those in a higher position and consideration for those below. According to Kong Fuzi, in this way, the correct behavior of the ruler helps establish a society of virtuous people, as each citizen aspires to become a morally "superior person."

FIVE CONSTANT RELATIONSHIPS

Kong Fuzi outlined five essential relationship pairings that serve as shorthand for all human relationships.

Sovereign–subject Rulers should be benevolent and considerate to subjects, who should be loyal and respectful in return.

Father–son Parents should be loving and protective; their children should be obedient and polite in return.

Husband–wife Husbands should be good and fair; their wives should be dutiful and understanding in return.

Elder brother–younger brother Elder siblings should be gentle and caring; younger siblings should look up to them.

Friend–friend Elder friends should be kind and considerate; younger friends should be deferential to their elder friends in return.

2. The virtues are dispersed

The virtues displayed by the ruler are emulated by those they come into contact with. They are passed on and spread through the population.

3. The virtues of the people

The people imitate the leader's behavior and cultivate those virtues in themselves. In the process, they provide an example for each other.

The art of ruling

While the early political philosophers emphasized the need for wisdom and virtue in a ruler, the Renaissance thinker Niccolò Machiavelli argued that the art of ruling demands more practical qualities.

Political realism

In *The Prince* (1532), a political treatise in the form of a handbook for rulers, Italian diplomat Machiavelli (1469–1527) completely shifted the focus of political thinking. Rather than identifying the attributes that a ruler needs in order to foster the people's moral well-being or considering how society should be led in an ideal world, Machiavelli put morality aside. Instead, he offered a more realistic description of ruling in the world as it actually is and focused on the practical aspects of governing.

Due to his advocacy for somewhat unscrupulous methods, "Machiavellian" became a byword for political deviousness, but the move from morality to pragmatism in political theory was hugely influential, inspiring the more acceptable notion of *realpolitik* (practical politics). Machiavelli proposed that the outcomes of a ruler's actions—for the people, the state, and the leader themselves—are of utmost importance.

At the core of Machiavelli's revolutionary approach to the art of ruling was the idea that there is a difference between personal and political morality. The responsibilities of a ruler are different from those of people in everyday life: for the good of the state and its people, it is often necessary for a ruler to act in a way that would be considered unethical in other

The end justifies the means

Machiavelli was one of the first philosophers to argue that the morality of an action should be judged by its outcome rather than its principles, especially in matters to do with political leadership. In effect, he said that for a ruler, the end justifies the means.

Decisive

Machiavelli advised that a ruler should be either "a true friend or a downright enemy" to gain respect. It is better to be decisive and take one side than be neutral.

circumstances. According to Machiavelli, what matters is the outcome—the bigger picture. This necessitates a particular set of political skills, very different from the wisdom and morality advocated for previously.

To govern effectively, a ruler has to be prepared to break with conventional morality—using manipulation, bribery, deception, and even violence to retain power and supremacy and to earn the respect of the people. Asked whether it is better for a ruler to inspire love or fear in their subjects, Machiavelli answered that ideally they should do both, but if there has to be a choice, it is safer to be feared than to be loved.

LUDWIG VON ROCHAU

The term *realpolitik* was coined by the German writer Ludwig von Rochau (1810–73). Something of a firebrand, he was jailed as a student for his part in an uprising in Frankfurt in 1833. He escaped and lived in exile in France and Italy, working as a travel writer before returning to Germany, where he became a political journalist. In 1853, von Rochau wrote his seminal treatise *Principles of Realpolitik*. He later served as a member of the first Reichstag—German parliament—where he represented the National Liberal Party.

"**It is** necessary **for a** prince **wishing to hold his own to** know how to do wrong **and to** make use of it or not according to necessity."

Niccolò Machiavelli, *The Prince* (1532)

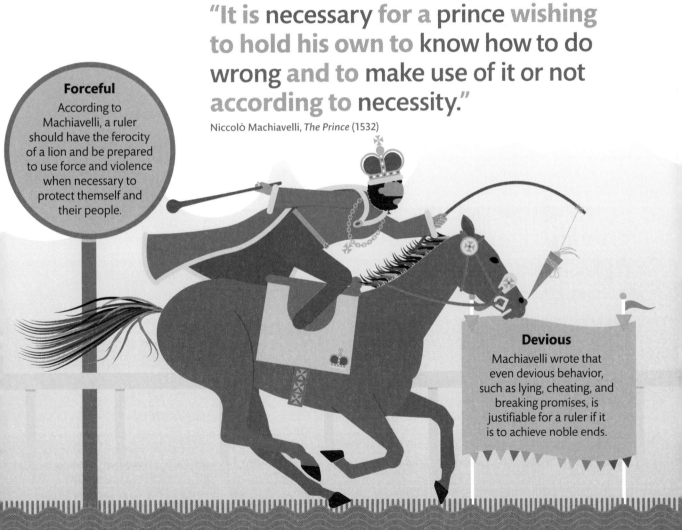

Forceful

According to Machiavelli, a ruler should have the ferocity of a lion and be prepared to use force and violence when necessary to protect themself and their people.

Devious

Machiavelli wrote that even devious behavior, such as lying, cheating, and breaking promises, is justifiable for a ruler if it is to achieve noble ends.

Choosing leaders

As well as identifying the character and skills required of a good leader, people also need a method of ensuring that these leaders are chosen to rule.

Passing down power

In early societies, leaders emerged naturally from the people. In many cases, these leaders established a tradition of nominating their successor, typically from the next generation of their own family. As communities evolved into city-states and nations, the practice of handing down the right to rule was often maintained. Monarchs of nations were seen as the heads of ruling families, and their right to rule was accepted. As power was passed down from generation to generation, dynasties became established: children were born to rule, and some rulers even believed themselves to have been divinely appointed.

From the 18th century onward, the majority of monarchies were overthrown and replaced with governments whose right to rule was established by military force or via the choice of the citizens, using a system of voting.

Other than a handful of absolute monarchs (see pp.70–71), the few remaining kings and queens now have only limited powers, which are granted to them by the elected government in what is known as a constitutional monarchy.

However, in many cases, the notion of a ruling class has not completely disappeared. Aristocrats, generals, and other powerful people often claim entitlement to power, not through birth but because of educational, financial, or other advantageous influences. Even in democracies, elected leaders are often drawn from a professional political class. In the late 20th century, democracies including the United States and Singapore had father and son leaders.

Born to rule?

Historically, the most common kind of leadership has been a hereditary monarchy, whether the title of the ruler was king, queen, emperor, or sultan. In the modern era, however, the idea of rule as a birthright has been largely replaced by rule by elected leadership.

> "The right of voting... is the primary right by which other rights are protected."
>
> Thomas Paine, political writer, *Dissertation on First Principles of Government* (1795)

HOW TO REMOVE A LEADER

In democracies, leaders can be voted out of office by the electorate, but there are other ways to bring about a change of rule.

> **Revolution** by citizens, often involving violent protest, has been used to world-changing effect, especially against tyrannical rulers.

> **Coups** are a threat in nations where the government falls out of favor with the leaders of its armed forces.

> **Regime change by an external power** is uncommon, but it may sometimes happen that one state removes another state's leader by instigating a revolution, coup, or military invasion.

Aristocracy

The relatives of monarchs have often been given titles and some limited local power. Similar honors have also sometimes been bestowed on people who have been of use to the monarch.

Electorate

In democracies, the people have a say in who should be their leader: citizens are entitled to vote in an election to decide who will represent their interests.

Line of succession

A monarch's position has almost always been hereditary, with power passing from one generation to the next. The line of succession has usually been from father to eldest son.

Hereditary power

In many societies, the monarch was believed to have been chosen by God, with a divine right to rule—what the ancient Chinese called the "mandate of heaven."

Elected representatives

In a democracy, the president or prime minister and their government are elected not simply to rule but to represent the views and wishes of the people.

The will of the people

Jean-Jacques Rousseau's notion of government by "the will of the people" has been realized in the many democratic countries that exist today.

A say in government

The idea that citizens should have a say in how their society is governed is an old one, and a form of democracy—or rule by the people—was established in the city-state of Athens in ancient Greece. But traditional ideas about rule by an all-powerful monarch persisted, and it is only since the 18th and 19th centuries that citizens have truly begun to have a political voice.

The extending of power from an elite to the people has been a gradual process. In many early democracies, only a particular class was given the right to vote, such as property-owning men—women got the vote much later (see pp.130–31)—but today, democracy generally involves the participation of all adult citizens.

Elected officials

With nations numbering often tens of millions of citizens, it is clearly impractical for every single person to participate directly in the decision-making process—proposing, debating, and voting on legislation, a system known as direct

Types of democracy

The original democracy was a form of direct democracy, in which eligible citizens voted on each issue before a decision was made. However, as the size of the electorates grew and the decisions to be made grew more complex, this proved impracticable, and instead a form of representative democracy evolved.

DIRECT DEMOCRACY

4. New law selected

The proposal selected directly by the majority of the citizens becomes law.

OPTION A   OPTION B

3. Choosing new legislation

The votes of the citizens are counted, and the decision of the majority determines which proposals are adopted.

2. No intermediaries

The citizens vote on specific proposals for laws rather than voting for a person or a party to make those decisions on their behalf. In this way, citizens have a direct say in legislation.

1. The role of the citizens

When a new law is proposed, all eligible citizens are invited to debate the issue and to vote for or against it.

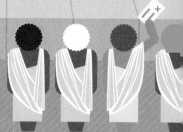
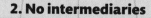

ANCIENT ATHENS

The first-ever democracies were established in ancient Greece. Historians believe that several city-states in the region adopted democratic constitutions, but the best known of these is Athens. After the tyrant Hippias was overthrown in 510 BCE, Cleisthenes, his successor as leader of Athens, introduced reforms, including a form of direct democracy. This was limited to only a select section of the male citizens, but nevertheless, it gave them a say in the government of the city-state. Eligible citizens met on a hill above the city to debate and vote.

democracy. And so, almost invariably nations have adopted some form of representative democracy.

Under this system, citizens vote to elect a person, or persons, to act on their behalf and represent their interests.

In a representative democracy, candidates put themselves forward for election and campaign on a range of issues and policies, often aligning themselves with a political party or a particular ideology. Citizens generally vote for the candidate who best represents their own views. Increasingly, these elected representatives are members of a class of professional politicians.

Less than half of the world's population lives in a fully democratic nation.

Economist Intelligence Unit (2020)

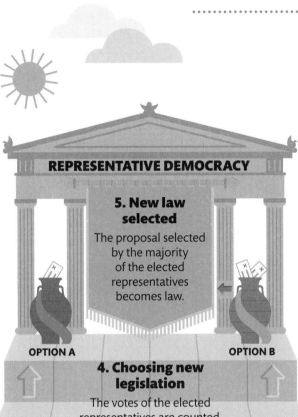

REPRESENTATIVE DEMOCRACY

5. New law selected

The proposal selected by the majority of the elected representatives becomes law.

OPTION A   OPTION B

4. Choosing new legislation

The votes of the elected representatives are counted, and the decision of the majority determines which proposals are adopted.

3. Representatives vote

When a new law is proposed, the elected representatives debate the issue and vote.

2. Representatives selected

The number of votes in favor determines which candidates are elected to act on behalf of the citizens.

1. The role of the citizens

Citizens are periodically invited to vote in elections for people or parties to represent their interests.

POLITICAL THEORY

Political ideologies

All political parties, groups, and movements are underpinned by an ideology, or set of commonly held ideas, beliefs, and principles. These ideas outline how a party believes society should be organized and how power should be distributed within a country or state. A party's ideology will be reflected in its core social, political, and cultural values and how it views such matters as the role of government, the economy, social welfare, and civil liberties.

Two axes

A political "spectrum" plots ideologies on a horizontal axis, with communism on the far left and fascism on the far right. However, an ideology can be economically left-wing but socially conservative. A political "compass," which adds a vertical axis from authoritarian to libertarian, therefore allows a subtler positioning.

✓ NEED TO KNOW

> **Authoritarian** political standpoints favor strict, rigid adherence to one authority at the expense of personal freedom.

> **Libertarian** political standpoints favor complete freedom of choice and individual rights. Libertarianism lies in absolute opposition to authoritarianism.

> **"Left" and "right"** originate from the French Revolution (1789–99) when revolutionaries sat to the left of the National Assembly and monarchists sat to the right.

Communism
This left-wing ideology (see pp.54–55) emphasizes collective responsibility rather than individual freedoms, which brings it closer to authoritarianism than libertarianism.

Socialism
This center-left viewpoint states that people should collectively own the main means of producing wealth and control it democratically (see pp.52–53).

Social democracy
This centrist ideology contains some socialist principles but believes that capitalism can be reformed and made fairer for all citizens (see pp.56–57).

LEFT

Libertarian socialism
This far-left socialist ideology is anti-authoritarianism and anti-state, and rejects hierarchy (see pp.42–43).

Anarchism
This far-left, extreme-libertarian ethos rejects governments, hierarchies, and capitalism and advocates for individual rights and responsibilities (see pp.44–45).

CORE VALUES

Political ideologies can be difficult to define precisely. Even those within the same grouping vary. As a general rule, opposing ideologies have opposing views. Both left- and right-wing ideologies have some core values.

Left

Ideologies, such as communism and socialism, favor equal rights, social justice, public ownership, and provision of welfare funded via taxation.

Right

Ideologies, such as conservatism, adhere to private enterprise, competition, individual freedom, social order, and minimal state interference.

> "... no system, not even the most inhuman, can continue to exist without an ideology."
>
> Joe Slovo, South African politician

AUTHORITARIAN

Nationalism
This ethos, often linked to right-wing politics, with strong elements of authoritarianism, puts the importance of the nation above that of the individual (see pp.48–49).

Fascism
Positioned at the far right of the political spectrum, fascism is a highly authoritarian ideology that places value on a strictly regimented society (see pp.46–47).

Conservatism
A middling right-wing ideology, conservatism places value on traditional power structures and a paternalistic approach to change (see pp.38–39).

RIGHT

Liberalism
Sitting close to the libertarian axis, liberalism is a political ideology that advocates for the protection of an individual's rights and freedoms, but not at a cost to others (see pp.36–37).

Libertarianism
A right-wing political philosophy, libertarianism upholds people's freedom and individualism with minimal interference from the state (see pp.42–43).

Anarcho-capitalism
Sitting at the extreme right of the political spectrum, anarcho-capitalism combines some of the libertarian elements of anarchism with support for free-market capitalism (see pp.44–45).

LIBERTARIAN

 Liberalism

Encompassing a broad range of political and philosophical ideas, liberalism is based on principles of equality and liberty. Humans have basic rights that must be protected, provided they do no harm.

Rights and freedoms

Liberalism is a political movement deeply rooted in ideas of social justice, social reform, and civil and human rights. Socially and politically, supporters of liberalism are committed to freedom of speech, democracy, tolerance, and equality before the law. As a movement, liberalism is reformist rather than revolutionary and is often regarded as progressive, with a proven record of backing social causes, such as the rights of women, disabled people, and LGBTQ+ individuals.

Liberalism emerged in the 17th and 18th centuries as a challenge to the long-held belief in hereditary privilege and the "divine right" of kings. English philosopher John Locke laid its foundations when he argued that humans have natural rights that are universal and inalienable (see pp.16–17)— these principles were later incorporated into the constitutions of the US and France. A later English philosopher, Jeremy Bentham (1748–1832), who was the founder of utilitarianism (see box), contributed to liberalism by arguing that decisions should be made on the principle of achieving the greatest happiness for the greatest number.

One of the most significant liberal thinkers of the time was John Stuart Mill (1806–73). An English philosopher and economist, he advocated for democratically elected governments whose role was to protect the rights of the individual. Mill believed that government had a social role in health, education, and mitigating poverty. This type of social liberalism was influential, particularly in

Personal freedom
According to Mill, an individual should be allowed to play music whenever they like, and as loudly as they want to. They are free to act as they please.

The harm principle

John Stuart Mill believed that each individual should be free to live life as they please, provided they do no harm to others. This is known as Mill's "harm principle." In his essay *On Liberty* (1859), Mill said that the only justification for an authority to limit an individual's actions would be to prevent harm to others. On this basis, for instance, a government would be justified in imposing noise restrictions.

Harm to others
However, one person's actions, such as playing music too loudly, may impinge on or cause harm to someone else, who has the right to enjoy peace and quiet.

Britain, where liberal politician William Beveridge (1879–1963) published his 1942 report laying the basis for the welfare state, which was implemented in 1948.

Economic liberalism

Economically, liberalism favors a capitalist free market, free trade and competition, and the private ownership of industries and property. This approach was developed by Scottish economist Adam Smith (1723–90), whose influential 1776 work *The Wealth of Nations* argued for a free-market economy that would

allow the laws of supply and demand to find their own level. Later, liberal economists, notably John Maynard Keynes (1883–1946), argued that governments should intervene in times of economic hardship.

Liberalism has influenced government policies in many Western democracies. Recently, some countries have witnessed the rise of neoliberalism (see pp.40–41), which supports extreme free-market economies, and libertarianism (see pp.42–43), which argues for unrestrained personal liberties.

Restrictions to protect
If someone's actions cause harm, that person's freedom should be limited, and society has a duty to do this. For instance, local authorities may impose noise regulations.

BENTHAM AND MILL'S UTILITARIANISM

Utilitarianism is a theory of morality that promotes actions that cause happiness and opposes actions that cause harm. Jeremy Bentham believed that happiness could be measured with a "Hedonic Calculus" (an algorithm for calculating pleasure). He argued that the right course of action is one that leads to the happiness of the greatest number of people: the concept of the "greatest good." John Stuart Mill supported this principle but was concerned about its political implications. He worried that it could allow a tyrannical majority rule that dismissed the happiness of minority groups. Instead, he advocated for laws that gave all people the freedom to pursue happiness.

A balance of freedoms
Restrictions allow both people to live harmoniously: if one person can only play music at certain times or volumes, this means the other person's life is not interfered with.

"The liberty of the individual **must be thus far** limited; **he must not make himself** a nuisance to other people."

John Stuart Mill, *On Liberty* (1859)

Conservatism

Conservatives believe in the importance of traditional social and political structures and strive to preserve them. Their key values are law and order, gradual change, and belief in a governing class.

Gradual change

Modern conservatism emerged in the 18th century, partly as a reaction to the upheavals of the French Revolution, which began in 1789. The following year, Irish statesman Edmund Burke (1729–97) published a highly influential political pamphlet titled *Reflections on the Revolution in France*. In this, he deplored the rapid destruction of social structures in France and the revolutionaries' attempts to replace the wisdom accumulated by previous generations with abstract ideas of "liberty, fraternity and equality." Burke recognized that social change might be needed, but he rejected revolution. Instead, he argued that change should evolve gradually. Burke's theories remain central to the political ideology of modern conservatism.

Structured society

For conservatives, society is naturally hierarchical, and the rule of law is vital to ensure order and stability. Governments tend to be interventionist, looking after the good of the nation. Conservatives support the idea of a ruling elite, made up of the most experienced and best equipped to lead. Once, this would have been a privileged hereditary class; today, it is more likely to comprise well-educated professionals and financiers. Conservatism favors capitalism and promotes private industry, enterprise, free trade, and the

Religion

Organized religion is highly regarded by conservatives for its traditional values, which reinforce stability and order and provide a moral compass.

> **"I am a Conservative to preserve all that is good in our constitution... I seek to preserve property and to respect order."**
>
> Benjamin Disraeli, former British prime minister, taken from a speech at High Wycombe, UK (1832)

Conservative values

Underpinning conservatism is a belief in a hierarchical social order rather than equality. In such a society, the rule of law is vital to preserve order and prevent anarchy. Conservatives believe in maintaining traditional values that have evolved over time. If change is necessary, it should be implemented gradually.

Traditional family structure

Conservatives value traditional family structures. They are seen as stable and sharing common values that contribute to social order.

creation of wealth, which it believes will "trickle down" to the less well off. Conservative governments play a limited role in trade, industry, and, increasingly, in welfare provision.

Socially and culturally, conservatism promotes the value of traditional institutions and processes.

Worldwide conservatism

In practice, conservatism can vary from liberal to more authoritarian forms. Most modern Western European conservative parties tend to be economically conservative but may be socially liberal, recognizing, for example, same-sex civil partnerships. In the US, however, modern conservatism is closely linked to the right-wing Republican Party, which believes in small government and traditional values. In India, the Bharatiya Janata Party (BJP) represents conservative politics, promoting cultural nationalism and a conservative social and economic policy. In the 21st century, Russia has also pursued conservative policies in social, cultural, and political matters.

Private property

A core conservative belief is the right to own property. Conservatism supports laws that protect inherited wealth and properties.

Work ethic

Conservatives believe in success through hard work and personal responsibility rather than reliance on the state.

Hierarchical society

While most conservatives would not support hereditary power, they believe in an elite class that is best qualified to rule.

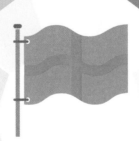

Patriotism

Not all conservatives are nationalistic; however, conservatism encourages a love of country and the idea of shared national values.

Paternalistic government

Paternalistic conservatism emphasizes state intervention to cultivate a good life for all of its citizens.

Neoliberalism

The ideology of neoliberalism stands for meritocracy, minimal government, low taxation, privatization, deregulation, and free-market economics.

Free markets

The roots of neoliberalism lie in the ideas of the 18th-century philosopher Adam Smith, who argued that free markets are the best means of ensuring wealth is distributed fairly in society.

However, neoliberalism is a 20th-century philosophy that was developed in opposition to the policies of state intervention pursued in Europe and the US during the Great Depression and the period that followed World

War II. One of the first proponents of neoliberalism was Austrian economist Friedrich Hayek (1899–1992), who argued that free markets respond directly to individual needs and so deliver benefits to society much more

Rolling back the state

Neoliberals argue that the state should play only a minimal role in managing a nation's affairs. This is in sharp contrast to the post–World War II view that the state should pay for a range of public services, including education, transportation, and healthcare. They also claim that economies stagnate when governments spend too much money on public utilities and services, which instead should be run as businesses by private companies.

The privatization of public services

According to neoliberalist theory, social services, such as healthcare and education, and public utilities, such as transportation, prisons, and postal services, should be privatized in order to save public money and increase economic efficiency.

The minimal state

In neoliberalist systems, individuals should be free to pursue their own goals and so should be free from state interference. The state's role should therefore be limited to ensuring that the market is operating freely.

FOR SALE

SOLD
WATER SERVICES

HEALTHCARE

✓ NEED TO KNOW

> **Deregulation** is the reduction of governmental control, such as removing laws, often in particular industries.

> **Privatization** is the transfer of a business or service from public to private ownership and control.

> **Meritocracies** are political systems in which people are awarded success or power on the basis of ability.

> **Free markets** are economic systems based on supply and demand with little or no government intervention.

efficiently than the state. Another neoliberal thinker was US economist Milton Friedman (1912–2006), who argued that a key role of government is to control the money supply.

The neoliberal world

Neoliberals claim that individuals should be responsible for themselves and that the role of government is to oversee economic growth rather than spend money on public services. In the 1980s, British prime minister Margaret Thatcher and President Ronald Reagan put this philosophy into practice, fomenting a period of social unrest. They privatized public services, deregulated businesses and banks, reduced taxes, and also cut government spending on essential social services.

Neoliberalism has since been adopted by many countries around the world and now influences the policies of global institutions, such as the International Monetary Fund and the World Bank (see pp.164–65). However, its critics argue that although it has made bankers, financiers, and global corporations extremely rich, it has also resulted in widespread income inequality.

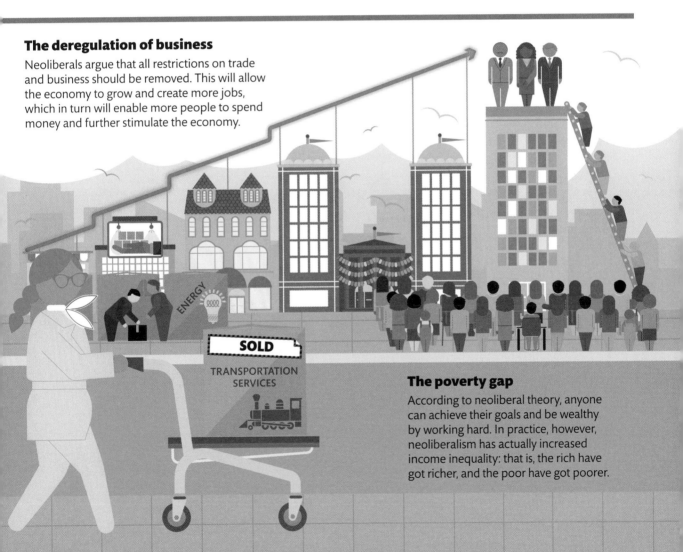

The deregulation of business

Neoliberals argue that all restrictions on trade and business should be removed. This will allow the economy to grow and create more jobs, which in turn will enable more people to spend money and further stimulate the economy.

ENERGY

SOLD

TRANSPORTATION SERVICES

The poverty gap

According to neoliberal theory, anyone can achieve their goals and be wealthy by working hard. In practice, however, neoliberalism has actually increased income inequality: that is, the rich have got richer, and the poor have got poorer.

Libertarianism

Individualism and freedom of choice lie at the heart of libertarianism, a political philosophy that unites both the extreme left and the extreme right in opposing state interference.

Individual liberty

Libertarianism has its origins in the ideas of classical liberal thinkers, such as John Locke and John Stuart Mill (see pp.36–37). However, it also has left- and right-wing traditions, which have appeared more recently.

The left-wing tradition has its roots in the writings of the 19th-century anarchists (see pp.44–45) and libertarian socialists. One of the earliest uses of the term "libertarian" was in 1895, when French anarchist Sébastien Faure (1858–1942) started publishing his journal *Le Libertaire* (The Libertarian). A more recent left-wing libertarian was the American environmentalist Murray Bookchin (1921–2006). His ideas shaped both the anti-globalization movement and the Occupy movement, which began in the US in October 2011 before spreading worldwide. Coining the slogan "We are the 99%," the Occupy movement attacked crony corporatism and corrupt financiers and highlighted the glaring inequalities between the very rich (the 1 percent) and the rest of society (the 99 percent).

Right-wing libertarianism

In recent years, a right-wing version of libertarianism has also become influential, particularly

CASE STUDY

The Free State Project

In 2001, Jason Sorens, then a student at Yale Univesity, founded a libertarian movement known as the Free State Project. He encouraged American libertarians to move to the state of New Hampshire, believing that 20,000 "movers" would be sufficient to begin the process of changing the political culture of the state. The ultimate goal of the project is for libertarians to take over the New Hampshire government and to start running it according to libertarian principles. To date, over 5,000 libertarians have migrated to the state.

Individualism and liberty

Libertarians share a mistrust of government, but many disagree on the question of how individual liberties should be protected. Left-wing libertarians claim that capitalism creates inherently unequal societies, whereas right-wing libertarians argue that only capitalism frees people to live in the way they wish.

Capitalism

Left-wing libertarians want to be free of capitalism, which they argue infringes personal liberty by generating inequality.

in the US. Right-wing libertarians are anti-egalitarian and support capitalism, free-market enterprise, and the rights of private ownership. Influenced by the American philosopher Robert Nozick (1938–2002), many right-wing libertarians argue that taxation is theft and that whatever a person produces, owns, or inherits should be theirs and theirs alone. An example of right-wing libertarianism was the Tea Party movement, which appeared in the US in 2009. Conservative voters congregated at mass gatherings known as "tea parties," at which they demanded that President Obama's healthcare law be scrapped and the national debt reduced by cutting back on social spending.

> "Libertarians are self-governors in both personal and economic matters."
>
> Advocates for Self-Government, libertarian organization (1995)

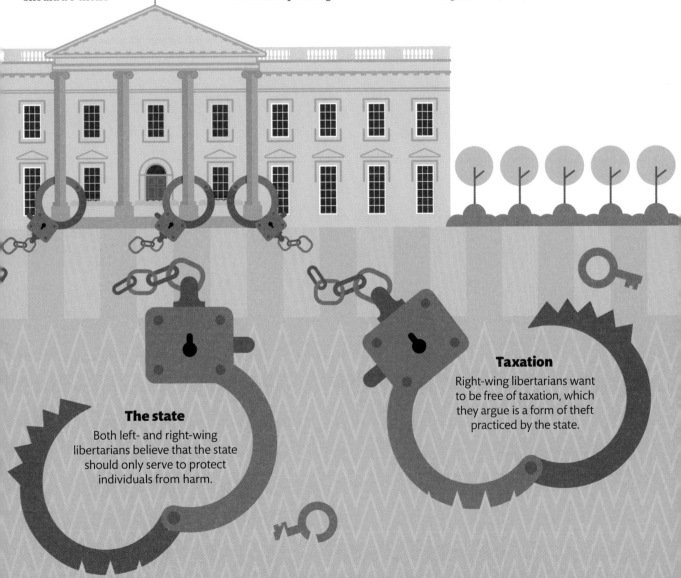

The state
Both left- and right-wing libertarians believe that the state should only serve to protect individuals from harm.

Taxation
Right-wing libertarians want to be free of taxation, which they argue is a form of theft practiced by the state.

Anarchism

The origins of the word *anarchism* lie in the ancient Greek term *anarkhia*, meaning "without rulers." In practice, it means the rejection of political authority. Anarchists believe the people themselves should make the rules.

Rule from the bottom up

Anarchists value personal liberty above all and stand against any form of authority that threatens an individual's freedom. They view the state as oppressive and believe it rules by coercion. To them, even democratically elected rulers are illegitimate. Anarchists favor the abolition of the state, leaving people free to organize themselves in self-governing groups, free from any form of political, economic, or social hierarchies. Anarchism is often associated with the far-left axis of the political spectrum, but it can also appeal to those on the right. Anarcho-capitalism combines libertarian (see pp.42–43) elements of anarchism with support for free-market capitalism.

Forms of anarchism

Anarchist ideas vary broadly between being focused on individuals or cooperative groups and between left versus right. On the left, mutualism and anarcho-syndicalism would replace the state with increasingly left-wing policies. On the right, anarcho-capitalists oppose the state but not free markets, property, or the rule of law.

Ending the state
At the heart of anarchism is the abolition of the state. Anarchists believe the state is inherently corrupt because it will always act in the interest of a ruling elite.

Individual anarchism
A person believes in retreating from civil society and living according to their own conscience, unconstrained by the authority of others.

Mutualism
Providing a link between individual and social anarchism, mutualism emphasizes social equality, trade unions, and mutual (members-owned) banks with zero-interest loans.

Theory and practice

Anarchism is built on the ideas of Enlightenment philosophers, such as Jean-Jacques Rousseau (see pp.12–13), who believed that people are good and that the state deprives them of their natural freedoms. Pierre-Joseph Proudhon (1809–65), French philosopher and first self-declared anarchist, said that "property is theft." Russian revolutionary Peter Kropotkin (1842–1921) fused communism and anarchism to form anarcho-communism. He argued for the abolition of private property in favor of common ownership and for replacing the state with direct democracy.

There are small-scale examples where anarchism has been put into practice. In Spain before the Civil War (1936–1939), anarchists set up self-governing communities, but the experiment was cut short when the country fell to fascist rule. The communal-living *kibbutz* movement in Israel was inspired by anarchist ideas of self-management, and Christiana, a commune of close to 1,000 people in Copenhagen, has operated outside Danish authority since 1971.

Anarchist principles can also be seen in modern anti-globalization and environmental movements, such as the direct-action group Extinction Rebellion.

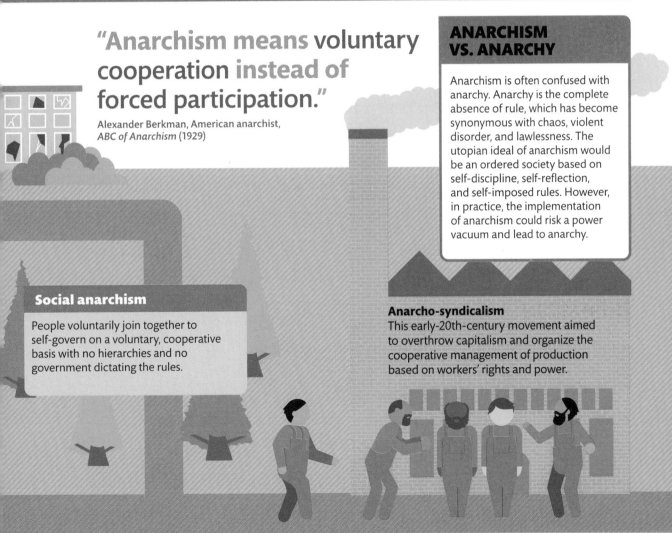

"**Anarchism means** voluntary cooperation **instead of** forced participation."

Alexander Berkman, American anarchist,
ABC of Anarchism (1929)

ANARCHISM VS. ANARCHY

Anarchism is often confused with anarchy. Anarchy is the complete absence of rule, which has become synonymous with chaos, violent disorder, and lawlessness. The utopian ideal of anarchism would be an ordered society based on self-discipline, self-reflection, and self-imposed rules. However, in practice, the implementation of anarchism could risk a power vacuum and lead to anarchy.

Social anarchism

People voluntarily join together to self-govern on a voluntary, cooperative basis with no hierarchies and no government dictating the rules.

Anarcho-syndicalism

This early-20th-century movement aimed to overthrow capitalism and organize the cooperative management of production based on workers' rights and power.

Fascism

Sitting on the far right of the political spectrum, fascism is an extreme nationalist authoritarian ideology that prioritizes the power and unity of the state over the freedoms of individuals.

Restoring glory

Fascism dates back to the rise of nationalism in the late 19th century. The ideology gained momentum after World War I (1914–18), fueled by the political chaos that followed the conflict. Italy was the first country to become a fascist state. In 1919, Benito Mussolini (1883–1945) formed the Italian Fascist Party. Declaring that he would revive the glory of the Roman Empire, he seized power in 1922, later ruling as a dictator. Working closely with Italian businesses, Mussolini set out to restructure Italy's economy and expand its influence.

Fascism spread throughout Europe in the years that followed. In 1939, after a civil war, nationalist General Francisco Franco (1892–1975) seized power in Spain and ruled it as a fascist state, quashing all opposition. In neighboring Portugal, António de Oliveira Salazar (1889–1970) ruled as a dictator from 1932 to 1968, with his policies incorporating many fascist principles.

Fascism took a different form in Germany. Known as National Socialism or Nazism, it was advocated by Adolf Hitler, who gained support by exploiting the humiliation Germany felt after World War I. Nazism was deeply racist and anti-Semitic. Promoting the concept of a "pure" Aryan race, the Nazis committed genocide against the Jews and slaughtered many minority groups.

"All within the state, nothing outside the state, nothing against the state."

Benito Mussolini, Italian dictator (c.1920s)

State control

Fascism is nationalistic: the strength of the nation state takes precedence over the rights and freedoms of the individual. In Italy, the state restricted the press, only allowing media that expressed a "faithfulness to the Fatherland."

Regimented society
Strength in unity is a core fasci[...] principle. A fascist state is rigid[...] structured and hierarchical. Th[...] state controls all activity, including the economy.

NEOFASCISM

Today, no regime refers to itself as fascist. However, the term neofascist is often used to describe political parties or movements— such as the National Rally in France or Golden Dawn in Greece—whose ideologies resemble those of 20th-century fascist movements. In the US, white supremacist groups are countered by the "antifa," or anti-fascist, movement.

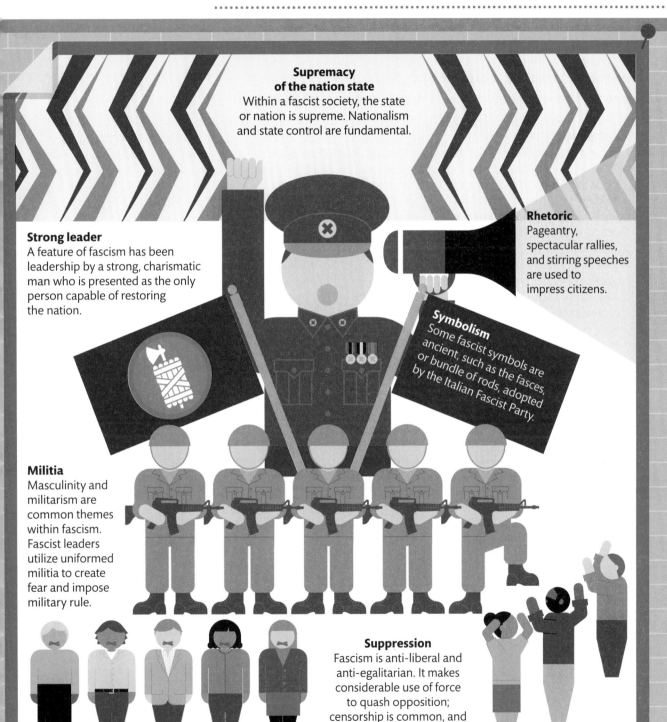

Supremacy of the nation state
Within a fascist society, the state or nation is supreme. Nationalism and state control are fundamental.

Strong leader
A feature of fascism has been leadership by a strong, charismatic man who is presented as the only person capable of restoring the nation.

Rhetoric
Pageantry, spectacular rallies, and stirring speeches are used to impress citizens.

Symbolism
Some fascist symbols are ancient, such as the fasces, or bundle of rods, adopted by the Italian Fascist Party.

Militia
Masculinity and militarism are common themes within fascism. Fascist leaders utilize uniformed militia to create fear and impose military rule.

Suppression
Fascism is anti-liberal and anti-egalitarian. It makes considerable use of force to quash opposition; censorship is common, and free speech is forbidden.

Nationalism

The goal of nationalism is to unite the people of a country under a single national identity in order to encourage support for the country and to promote its interests.

Shared identity

Nationalism is an ideology based on the idea that the nation and the state are one and that a nation should not only be self-governing but also free from the influence of other nations. It differs from patriotism, which is a love of one's country, regardless of the language, culture, or ethnic identity of its people.

Nationalists argue that the people of a country should celebrate their common identity as members of that country and so stand united against their enemies. However, in doing so, they may also encourage citizens to feel a sense of superiority over other nations and peoples.

What is a nation?

A nation is a community of people who live within a defined geographical area. Typically, the community shares a common language, culture, and ethnic heritage, but it may also be home to people from other cultures who share the nation's values. In liberal countries, the national identity transcends the ethnic differences of citizens. In less liberal countries, ethnicity may be a defining feature of the nation.

Since the late 18th century, nationalism has been a powerful driving force for change. It swept away France's monarchy during the French Revolution, which began in 1789, and became the rallying cry of the Risorgimento, the movement that unified the Italian states into a single state in 1861. Likewise, it underpinned the unification of Germany in 1871, when several German princedoms formed a nation-state.

Nationalism has also inspired numerous liberation movements that have fought to free

Soft borders
Interaction between nations is encouraged, and borders between them are either open or regulated.

LIBERAL NATIONALISM
Liberal nationalists celebrate the sense of shared identity that people feel on belonging to the same nation, regardless of their ethnicity.

Deportation
Depending on government attitudes, people perceived as not sharing a nation's values may be deported or refused entry.

countries from imperial control. In India, for example, it drove an independence movement that ended British colonial rule over the country in 1947. In Africa, similar movements inspired many states to claim independence from other colonial powers, such as France and Germany (see pp.60–61).

However, there is a darker form of nationalism, which encourages racism against minority ethnic groups within a nation and xenophobia against people from other countries, such as refugees and asylum seekers.

Rise of extremism

Extreme nationalism appears to be on the rise in the 21st century, with the emergence of far-right white supremacy movements in the US and Hindu nationalism in India. Such movements threaten to undermine the liberal ideals of nationalism (see below).

> "Nationalism is power hunger tempered by self-deception."
>
> George Orwell, British writer, *Notes on Nationalism* (1945)

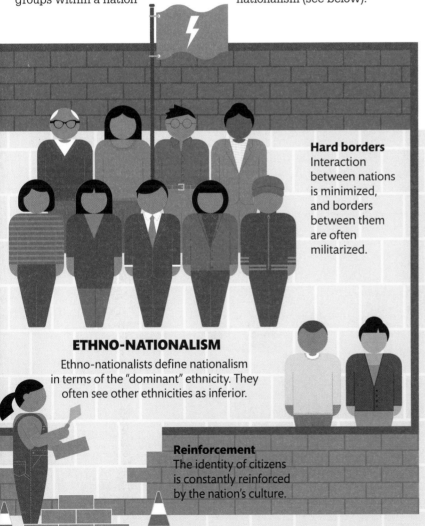

Hard borders
Interaction between nations is minimized, and borders between them are often militarized.

ETHNO-NATIONALISM
Ethno-nationalists define nationalism in terms of the "dominant" ethnicity. They often see other ethnicities as inferior.

Reinforcement
The identity of citizens is constantly reinforced by the nation's culture.

Marginalization
People who do not embrace the nation's culture can be seen as sympathizers for other cultures and so are often marginalized or treated as enemies.

CASE STUDY

Kurdish nationalism

Many states contain regions that are populated by peoples who have their own ethnic and cultural identities and so wish to build their own states. One such people are the Kurds, between 25 and 35 million of whom live in the mountains bordering Turkey, Syria, Iraq, Iran, and Armenia. The Kurds have been fighting to gain independence from these countries since 1920 but remain the largest stateless ethnic group in the world.

Populism

Populism effectively pits ordinary people against existing politicians, governments, or institutions, which are portrayed as elitist and corrupt. A charismatic leader typically presents themselves as the people's champion.

A divisive ideology

Some political scientists describe populism as a "thin ideology", because it rarely has or advocates for an economic or social program. Instead, it depends on being provocative and divisive. Populism is underpinned by the idea that society is split into two, often antagonistic, camps: "the people" and "the elite."

Populism has manifested in both left- and right-wing politics. Examples of left-wing populism include the Occupy movement, which highlighted economic and social hardship, coining the slogan "We are the 99%"; the Podemos party in Spain, which challenged the country's austerity measures; and former Venezuelan president Hugo Chávez. On the right, examples include former president Donald Trump, Hungary's prime minister Victor Orbán, and Nigel Farage, former leader of the United Kingdom Independence Party (UKIP), who claimed that the European Union (EU) was undemocratic and a threat to British sovereignty.

Populist themes

Lack of democracy is a common theme in populist discourse and is frequently used to attack perceived elites. Populist politicians are elected through the democratic process but may subsequently show little respect for democracy, as demonstrated when Trump refused to accept the result of the 2020 presidential election.

Populist politicians gain support by tapping into people's feelings of exclusion. A populist leader, who may not be a conventional politician, rallies support by stirring up prejudice and blaming others for social injustice. This blame may be directed at the sitting government, intellectuals, or the media, any of whom are presented as overriding people's rights and freedoms. Populism, particularly on the right, can be aligned with nationalism, enabling blame to be directed toward immigrants or minority ethnic groups within a country.

The people vs. the elite

According to populism, society is divided into two opposing groups: the "people" and the "elite." The people are considered to be pure, exemplary citizens, while the elite are portrayed as undemocratic, corrupt, and uninterested in the needs of the people.

The people

The people are presented as morally superior. However, rather than reflecting the whole of society, they are often from a particular social class or religious group.

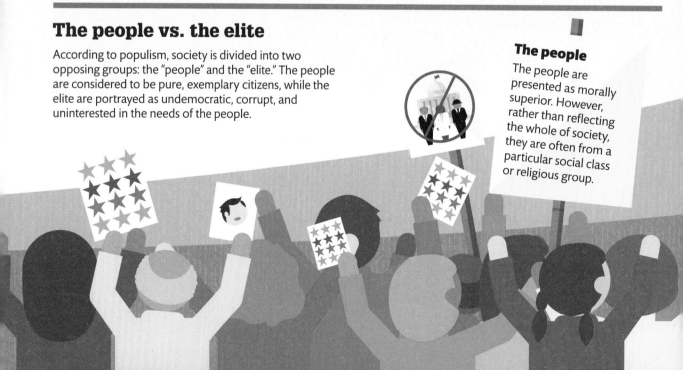

POPULISM IN THE 21ST CENTURY

In recent years, populist politicians have gained support in many countries. They have done so in response to various crises that have shaken the world, such as the financial crisis of 2007–08 and the displacement of millions of people due to wars in the Middle East. At such times, people are prone to seek easy answers to complicated problems and so are more easily swayed by politicians who prey on their anxieties about immigration and unemployment. Such crises also increase people's disillusionment with traditional politicians and political processes.

The charismatic leader

Claiming to represent the will of the people, populist leaders are skilled at whipping up a crowd. They are not necessarily aligned with a political party and are sometimes described as "demagogues."

The elite

Members of the elite are presented as corrupt and self-interested. They may be bankers, scientists, the media, intellectuals, or a sitting government.

 Socialism

Socialism is a range of political and economic theories that aim to end the exploitation of workers, ensuring that each person can enjoy the wealth created by their labor but only receive a share equal to their contribution.

Social justice

Socialism developed in the early 19th century in response to the growth of capitalism during the Industrial Revolution. German philosopher Karl Marx (1818–83) defined its principles, claiming that socialism was the first step toward communism (see pp.54–55). Socialists argue that the means of production must be regulated to protect workers from exploitation. Some socialists believe this is only possible if the means of production is transferred from private hands to public or state ownership. In a socialist country, each individual receives profits that reflect the size of their contribution. The state, as opposed to private enterprise, is often responsible for funding social

Challenging capitalism

Socialism sits on the left of the political spectrum. Fundamentally, it challenges the capitalist system, advocating for public ownership and cooperation over competition, private ownership, and private profits. Socialists strive for collective responsibility rather than the liberal emphasis on individual rights and freedoms.

Society is cooperative
Individuals work together and make decisions democratically. In the early and mid-1800s, "utopian" socialists experimented with self-sufficient communities.

Common ownership
The means of production—including tools, machinery, and factories—are collectively owned in many socialist societies, either by the state or by the workers in the form of cooperatives.

necessities, such as the provision of healthcare, education, housing, and energy, through a tax system.

Socialism has been profoundly influential, but its tenets have been open to interpretation. Revolutionary socialists argue for a seizure of power by the working class. Others believe that socialist policies can be achieved via elected governments that best reflect workers' interests.

"Socialism is their name for almost anything that helps all the people."

Harry S. Truman, former US president, New York speech (1952)

> ✓ **NEED TO KNOW**
>
> ❯ **Means of production** are the raw materials, tools, factories, and infrastructure needed to produce goods.
>
> ❯ **Capitalism** is a political system in which a country's trade and industry are controlled by private owners, rather than the state.

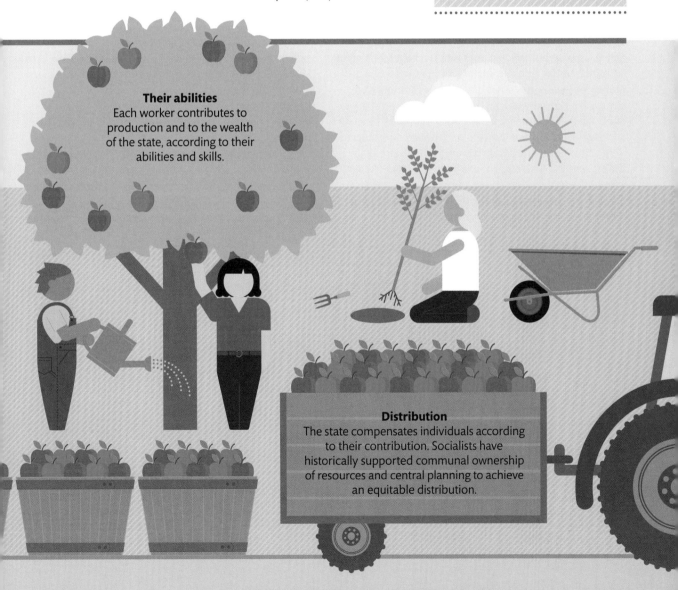

Their abilities
Each worker contributes to production and to the wealth of the state, according to their abilities and skills.

Distribution
The state compensates individuals according to their contribution. Socialists have historically supported communal ownership of resources and central planning to achieve an equitable distribution.

Communism

Communism is a political, social, and economic ideology that promotes the idea of a classless society, one in which private ownership does not exist and the state has withered away.

The Communist Manifesto

First described by the German philosophers Karl Marx (1818–83) and Friedrich Engels (1820–95) in *The Communist Manifesto* (1848), communism shares its anti-capitalist roots with socialism (see pp.52–53). However, Marx considered socialism to be only an intermediate stage on the path to communism.

Unlike socialists, communists envisage a society without social class, in which each person works for the good of everyone else, and all private property has been abolished. In a perfect communist system, the state's political and social institutions are rendered obsolete as society becomes capable of governing itself, without the coercive enforcement of the law. Engels described this process as the state "withering away." Marx believed that the only way to bring about communism was though revolution and that the workers of all countries had to unite and free themselves from capitalist oppression to create a world run by and for the working class.

Communism and revolution

Marx was writing during revolutionary times—there was a wave of political upheavals throughout Europe in 1848—but his political ideas only started to influence society in the 20th century.

In 1917, Russian Marxist Vladimir Ilich Ulyanov (1870–1924), better known as Lenin, led Russian industrial workers into a revolution to overthrow the czar (supreme ruler), establishing the world's first socialist state. Unlike Marx, Lenin believed in the importance of a "vanguard of revolutionaries"—a party of working-class socialists known as the Bolsheviks (from the Russian *bolshinstvo*, meaning "majority"), who would mobilize the proletariat into bringing down the ruling classes.

However, after the revolution, rather than introducing common ownership and creating a truly communist nation, the Bolsheviks took ownership of the machinery

Nobles

In the ancient and classical worlds, members of the ruling class were of noble birth. They owned the land and its workers and controlled laws.

Slaves

Workers in the ancient and classical worlds were often enslaved people. Their lives, bodies, labor, and the goods they produced were owned by the nobility.

Lords

Under the feudal system of medieval Europe, agricultural land was the main source of wealth. It was owned by lords, who inherited or were given the land by the monarch.

Serfs

A class of workers, or serfs, farmed the land. They were not slaves but had to work for the lords in exchange for a small amount of the produce they created.

of state. From 1924, under Lenin's successor, Joseph Stalin (1878–1953), the Soviet Union became a one-party dictatorship until its collapse in 1991.

In 1949, Mao Zedong (1893–1976) led a communist revolution in China. Other countries also adopted communist systems, and by 1980, around 1.5 billion people out of a global population of 4.4 billion were living in a country ruled by a communist political party.

Class struggle

For Marx, all history was the history of struggle and conflict between social classes. He adapted the ideas of German philosopher Georg Hegel (1770–1831), who stated that the only way to understand things is to see them as part of a march of historical progress that will ultimately lead to human freedom. For Marx, this state of "human freedom" was communism.

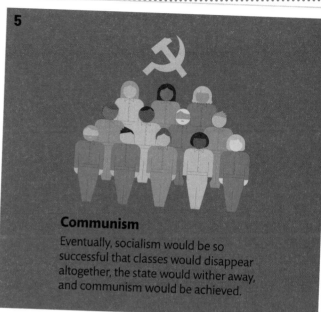

5

Communism
Eventually, socialism would be so successful that classes would disappear altogether, the state would wither away, and communism would be achieved.

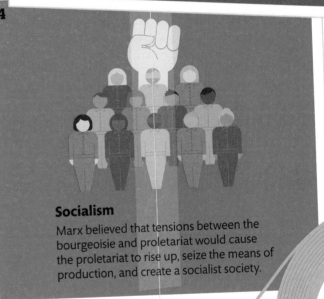

4

Socialism
Marx believed that tensions between the bourgeoisie and proletariat would cause the proletariat to rise up, seize the means of production, and create a socialist society.

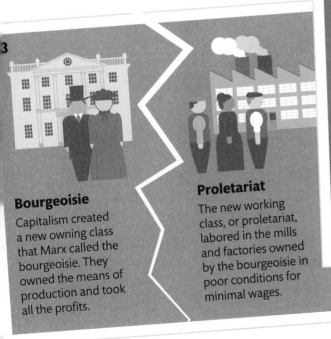

3

Bourgeoisie
Capitalism created a new owning class that Marx called the bourgeoisie. They owned the means of production and took all the profits.

Proletariat
The new working class, or proletariat, labored in the mills and factories owned by the bourgeoisie in poor conditions for minimal wages.

> "What the bourgeoisie... produces ... are its own grave-diggers."
>
> Karl Marx, *The Communist Manifesto* (1848)

Social democracy

Social democracy is a socialist ideology that is based on the belief that capitalism can be reformed, or humanized, to ensure comprehensive welfare provision for everybody.

Socialism and capitalism meet

The roots of social democracy lie in the ideas of German political theorist Eduard Bernstein (1850–1932), an associate of Karl Marx and Friedrich Engels. He suggested a new political system based on his interpretation of Marxism (see pp.52–55). His idea for social democracy incorporates similar values to socialism in that it aims to provide welfare for the disadvantaged, end inequality, and ultimately eradicate poverty. However, unlike socialism, social democracy does not seek to overthrow capitalism but rather to reform it and eliminate its worst injustices.

Social democracy favors a mixed economy that includes state-owned enterprises, particularly those providing public goods and services, such as health, education, and housing, alongside privately or partly state-owned businesses. Shareholders and workers manage these private businesses, which are closely regulated by the government. Social democracy sees taxation as a means of wealth distribution, the money raised being used to fund welfare and public services.

The Nordic model

The Nordic model describes the particular social democratic approach of the Nordic countries Denmark, Finland, Iceland, Norway, and Sweden to economic, social, and cultural policies. The model combines free-market capitalism with extensive social welfare provision, funded by high taxation rates.

Innovation

The Nordic model encourages innovation as a driver for economic growth. There is extensive investment into research and development, particularly in green technology.

Trade unions

Trade unions, employers, and the government work in partnership to set working conditions. Trade union membership is high—more than 90 percent in Iceland, for example.

Workforce participation

Workers participate in planning and decision making with employers. The two groups also meet in consultations with the government, which mediates on any points of conflict.

Social democratic parties of various kinds have been formed in most European countries. In the 1990s, social democratic ideas underpinned a political movement known as the "Third Way," which aimed to fuse liberal economics with social democratic welfare policies. It was a strand of politics favoured by US president Bill Clinton, in office from 1993 to 2001. Today, social democracy is most often associated with the Nordic countries, where implementation of the "Nordic model" has resulted in high standards of living for the majority of citizens.

DEMOCRATIC SOCIALISM

While social democracy includes elements of capitalism but combines them with a comprehensive welfare state, democratic socialism aims to transform the economy from a capitalist model to full socialism, in which the means of production is publicly owned. Democratic socialist parties include the Spanish left-wing populist party Podemos and the Greek left-wing party Syriza. In the US, former presidential candidate Bernie Sanders describes himself as a democratic socialist.

3 of the world's happiest countries from 2017 to 2019 were Nordic nations.

worldhappiness.report, "The Nordic Exceptionalism" (2020)

High taxes

Rates of taxation are among the highest in the world. Taxes are used to fund social benefits, such as free education and health care as well as guaranteed pensions.

Trust in government

Compared with other countries, populations in the Nordic countries have a higher degree of trust in their leaders. One reason could be the collective nature of the Nordic model.

Welfare state

A comprehensive welfare state is a fundamental aspect of the Nordic model. Big investment is put into so-called human capital, such as education, health, and childcare.

Multiculturalism

The history of humanity is one of migration. As a policy, multiculturalism seeks the integration of native and nonnative cultures within a state's sovereign borders.

The "melting pot"

The idea of multiculturalism is far from new. Since ancient times, there have been examples of cities and countries that have become home to different, ethnic, cultural, or religious groups. However, in recent decades, so many millions of people have immigrated to new countries (for economic reasons or to flee war, repression, or famine) that the ways in which countries accept immigrants has come under new scrutiny.

Until the mid-20th century, new arrivals to countries such as the US and the UK were expected to integrate into the dominant culture of their host country. This approach has been described as the "melting pot" because it anticipates that different cultures will eventually assimilate and blend into society, creating a uniform, homogenous culture. However, this approach has been criticized for valuing the host culture over immigrant cultures and for not doing enough to help immigrants integrate into their host country's culture. Critics even claim that the

Different approaches

In general, nations have followed one of two policies toward their ethnic minorities. The first is the melting pot approach, which encourages assimilation. The second is the multicultural, or salad bowl, approach, which embraces cultural diversity.

IDENTITY POLITICS

Multiculturalism arose out of a concern for the rights of people who were displaced from their countries during World War II. Since then, it has become associated with the idea of identity politics, which considers whether particular social groups, such as women, disabled people, and ethnic minorities, are disadvantaged by virtue of their identity alone (see pp.146–47). This approach ensures that the people within these groups influence the political agenda and that their specific rights are recognized. Critics argue that identity politics focuses too much on individual experience and that rights are universal, irrespective of an individual's identity.

Melting pot

This approach focuses on assimilating immigrants into the host country's "dominant" culture to create a homogenous society. It assumes that immigrants are always willing to abandon their traditional cultures.

melting pot approach is racist—in other words, that it is inherently hostile toward people of different ethnic backgrounds.

The "salad bowl"

An alternative to the melting pot approach is the multicultural, or "salad bowl," approach, which values diversity and seeks to support different cultures within a population. A multicultural society is one that enables people to retain their ethnic and cultural identity within the wider national culture.

In 1971, Canada became the first country to adopt multiculturalism as an official policy. This was

> ## "Multiculturalism is about the proper terms of relationship between different communities."
>
> Bhikhu Parekh, British political theorist, *Rethinking Multiculturalism* (2002)

codified in a 1988 Multiculturalism Act that states all citizens have the freedom to preserve, enhance, and share their cultural heritage. At the same time, however, Canada has been criticized for marginalizing its

Indigenous peoples (see pp.196–97). Multiculturalism was made an official national policy by Australia in 1973 and subsequently adopted by most European Union member-states.

Populace

The term "populace" refers to the people or population of a country. Due to the immigration of people over centuries, most of the world's countries include different ethnicities within their populations.

Salad bowl

This approach recognizes the diversity of immigrant populations. The host government passes laws that prevent discrimination against minority groups, who can preserve their cultural traditions.

Pan-Africanism

Pan-Africanism is a global ideology and movement that seeks to create a sense of solidarity and collaboration between all people of African descent, both within the African continent and among the worldwide African diaspora.

First stirrings

Also sometimes known as Black nationalism, Pan-Africanism advocates self-determination for those of Black African descent. Its roots lie in the struggles of African people against European colonialism and the slave trade (see pp.138–39).

Martin Delany (1812–1885), the son of an enslaved man, initiated the "Back to Africa" movement in the US. He argued that Black people would not prosper alongside white people and urged African Americans to form their own nation in West Africa. Jamaican political activist Marcus Garvey (1887–1940) supported the idea and called for unity between Africans on the African continent and in the diaspora.

A political movement

During the 20th century, Pan-Africanism emerged as a distinct political movement. In 1900, Trinidadian lawyer Henry Sylvester Williams (1867–1911) convened the first Pan-African Congress. It condemned racism and the theft of African lands and supported independence from colonial rule. In the late 1950s, the leader of newly independent Ghana, Kwame Nkrumah, became a figurehead for African liberation. In 1961,

French West Indian psychiatrist Frantz Fanon (1925–61) published *The Wretched of the Earth*, which examined the traumatic effects of colonialism and argued for African nations creating a "Third Way" of government rather than copying the West's democracy.

In 1963, Emperor Haile Selassie of Ethiopia delivered a landmark speech to the United Nations in which he said that until the idea that one race is superior and another inferior is abandoned, world peace will always be an illusion. The same year, 32 nations came together to form the Organization of African Unity (OAU), with the aims of encouraging political and economic integration and eradicating all traces of colonialism on the African continent. Around this time, Black liberation movements, such as the Black Panthers in the US, formed across the diaspora.

Pan-Africanism remains a powerful political force, aimed at unity and overcoming the legacy of European colonization. In a time of globalization, Pan-Africanism advocates seeking African solutions to African issues.

> **"Until all Africans stand and speak as free beings... the African continent will not know peace."**
>
> Emperor Haile Selassie, address to the United Nations (1963)

The pillars of Pan-Africanism

Pan-Africanism is a global political, cultural, and even religious movement—the religion of Rastafarianism focuses attention on the African diaspora and calls for its resettlement in the promised land of "Zion," or Africa. Pan-Africanism has also promoted Black pride, history, and cultural achievements, counteracting the prevailing Eurocentric view of history and politics.

NKRUMAH'S GHANA

Ghana played a significant role in the development of Pan-Africanism. Kwame Nkrumah (1909–1972) led the country to independence from Britain in 1957, becoming its first prime minister and president. In 1958, he hosted the first All-African Peoples' Conference in the Ghanaian capital, Accra. At the conference, representatives from 28 African nations called for unity in the liberation struggle and agreed that violence would be necessary in some cases. Nkrumah funded African liberation struggles and supported the American civil rights movement. Within Ghana, he also expanded education as a means of empowerment and to promote Pan-African ideology.

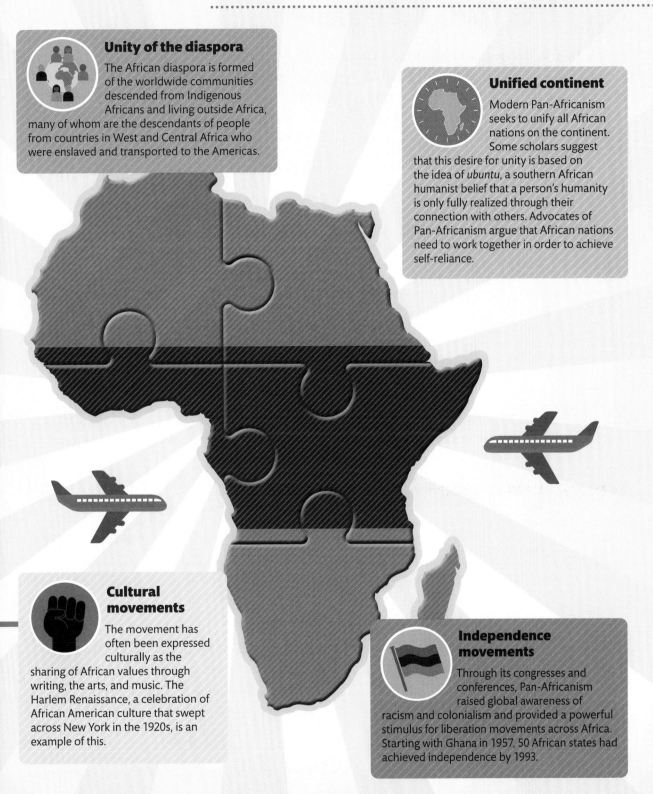

Unity of the diaspora

The African diaspora is formed of the worldwide communities descended from Indigenous Africans and living outside Africa, many of whom are the descendants of people from countries in West and Central Africa who were enslaved and transported to the Americas.

Unified continent

Modern Pan-Africanism seeks to unify all African nations on the continent. Some scholars suggest that this desire for unity is based on the idea of *ubuntu*, a southern African humanist belief that a person's humanity is only fully realized through their connection with others. Advocates of Pan-Africanism argue that African nations need to work together in order to achieve self-reliance.

Cultural movements

The movement has often been expressed culturally as the sharing of African values through writing, the arts, and music. The Harlem Renaissance, a celebration of African American culture that swept across New York in the 1920s, is an example of this.

Independence movements

Through its congresses and conferences, Pan-Africanism raised global awareness of racism and colonialism and provided a powerful stimulus for liberation movements across Africa. Starting with Ghana in 1957, 50 African states had achieved independence by 1993.

Feminism

Feminism is both an ideology and a movement. Its core aims include social, political, and economic equality of the sexes and an end to sexism and the oppression of women in all areas of society.

A wide-ranging ideology

Feminism challenges societies' views of sex and gender roles. The movement comprises many strands, which reflect the different perspectives on the causes of female oppression and how to overcome it. As a result, there are equal rights feminists, socialist feminists, Black feminists, radical feminists, intersectional feminists, and LGBTQ+ feminists amongst others.

Women have called for equal rights for centuries, but it was in the late 18th and early 19th centuries that their demands gained momentum. Notably, French activist Olympe de Gouges (1748–1793) and English writer Mary Wollstonecraft (1759–1797) argued that women deserved to be treated as equal citizens and needed to be freed from domestic tyranny (see pp.130–31).

In the mid-20th century, French writer Simone de Beauvoir (1908–1986) separated biological sex from gender, which she argued is a patriarchal idea that frames men as the norm and women as the "Other." She rejected "femininity" as a social construct that defines women as passive. Her ideas influenced American writer Betty Friedan (1921–2006), who argued that society conditioned women to conform to the idealized image of a housewife. Her 1963 book *The Feminine Mystique* inspired many white middle-class women to seek fulfillment outside the domestic realm.

Redefining feminism

In the late 20th century, some feminists reexamined the ways in which race, gender, class, and sexuality related to the movement. American writer bell hooks (1952–2021) accused feminism of marginalizing Black women and called for a new inclusive movement, while trans activists such as Julia Serano (1967–) have demanded the recognition of transgender women.

Early feminist campaigns focused on equal rights, particularly legal rights. Since then, feminists have analyzed and challenged every aspect of women's lives, including traditional family roles and violence against women, reproductive rights, sexuality, and racism.

CONTINUING INEQUALITIES

Feminism has achieved much for women and girls in many countries: the right to vote and own property, equal pay, entry into all areas of employment, and, perhaps most significantly, the recognition of sex and gender as political issues. However, despite more than 200 years of campaigning, glaring inequalities between women and men still exist. Some feminists blame the patriarchy—social structures and practices that facilitate male dominance—for this imbalance (see pp.142–43).

Worldwide, men earn 23 percent more than women, according to recent figures from the United Nations (UN). Women are also affected by gender bias at home: they do more unpaid work, such as childcare, than men. Violence against women remains endemic—worldwide, on average, 82 women every day die at the hands of former or current male partners, according to a 2018 report by the UN Office on Drugs and Crime (UNODC).

Four waves of feminism

The feminist movement has been divided into four metaphorical "waves." Feminism is a global movement, and critics of the "wave" approach argue that it focuses too much on white experience. It also suggests a linear progression, whereas feminism's ideas, values, and campaigns are complex and intertwined and have often overlapped.

THE FIRST WAVE

Rights
First-wave feminism emerged in the UK and the US in the late 19th and early 20th centuries. Its focus was on gaining the legal right to vote, to own property, and to have equal access to education.

"I'm a feminist... It'd be stupid not to be on my own side."
Maya Angelou, American author

THE SECOND WAVE

THE THIRD WAVE

THE FOURTH WAVE

Liberation from patriarchy
Gaining prominence in the late 1960s, second-wave feminism was synonymous with the Women's Liberation Movement. It challenged the patriarchy and women's social roles and explored sexualities and reasons for oppression.

Rebellion and race
In the 1990s, third-wave feminism emphasized individualism and rebellion, epitomized by punk rock "riot grrrls." A greater awareness of race led to the adoption of the theory of intersectionality (see pp.146–47).

Internet and inclusivity
The fourth wave began in 2010 on social media and focused on the empowerment of women and LGBTQ+ individuals. The #MeToo movement reached its height in 2017, highlighting male sexual assault of women.

Environmentalism

Environmentalism is both an ideology and a political movement focused on protecting and restoring the natural world and reducing the impact of harmful human activities.

Threat to life

Environmentalism spans a broad range of issues, including climate change, pollution and the disposal of waste, the impact of burning fossil fuels, deforestation, water scarcity, and wildlife conservation. Environmentalists search for sustainable alternatives to industrial processes, arguing that such processes have already caused serious damage and, if unchecked, will threaten the future of the planet.

Concern for the environment gathered pace in the 1960s. *Silent Spring* (1962) by biologist Rachel Carson (1907–64) highlighted the devastating impact of DDT insecticide use in farming, and by the 1970s, environmentalism was a political issue. The 1972 UN Conference on the Human Environment was the first global conference to make the environment a key concern. "Green" political parties began to emerge in New Zealand, Australia, Tasmania, Britain, and Germany. Pollution, toxic waste, genetically modified food, and deforestation drove environmental movements and protests worldwide, including the Global South (the regions of Latin America, Africa, Asia, and Oceania), where the impact has been greatest.

As evidence of global warming grew, environmentalists called for cuts to carbon emissions. The 2015 UN Paris Agreement committed to maintaining global temperature well below 2°C above preindustrial levels, and in 2021, the UN Climate Change Conference met in Scotland with the aim of reducing carbon emissions to net zero by 2030.

DEEP ECOLOGY

Inspired by Norwegian philosopher Arne Naess (1912–2009), deep ecology is an environmental philosophy that takes an eco-centric view and states that all living things have equal value. According to Naess, environmentalists must "not only protect the planet for the sake of humans, but also, for the sake of the planet itself, to keep ecosystems healthy for their own sake." Deep ecologists argue for noninterference in the natural world and oppose capitalism, advocating for an alternative social system based on harmony with the planet and sustainable environmental practices.

Overpopulation can put pressure on resources, such as space, clean water, and fuel. However, some argue that overconsumption of resources, particularly by Western nations, is a greater problem.

Waste products may go to landfills where they release methane or carbon dioxide—both greenhouse gases—into the atmosphere, or they may end up in the oceans.

Pollution occurs when chemicals are released into the air, water, or ground, where they can damage ecosystems.

Deforestation—the removal of large areas of trees—has a damaging effect on ecosystems. Between 1990 and 2016, more than 502,000 sq. miles (1.3 million sq. km) of forest were destroyed.

Burning fossil fuels, such as coal, oil, and gas, releases vast amounts of carbon dioxide into the atmosphere, causing global warming. As of 2021, a 1.5°C rise risks severe environmental damage.

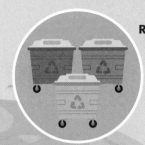

Recycling—producing new items from waste plastic, glass, metal, paper, and wood—reduces the need for new raw materials as well as reducing the amount of landfill and pollution.

Sustainable energy is a range of renewable sources of energy, such as wind, solar, and tidal power. They could replace fossil fuels.

Loss of biodiversity threatens the extinction of over one million animal and plant species worldwide.

Conserving biodiversity requires carefully managing and preserving natural habitats, nurturing local species, and banning pesticides.

Environmental threats and solutions

Many people today believe that humanity is facing an environmental crisis, including a climate emergency (see pp.192–93). Most people accept that threats to the environment have been caused by human activity, particularly over the last 200 years, with the emergence of fossil-fueled industrialization. Such threats include pollution, deforestation, lack of clean water, and a significant loss of biodiversity. Solutions to these issues are not straightforward; however, individuals can make a difference—for example, by reducing car and plane use, eating less meat and dairy, and recycling waste products. Environmentalists argue that governments and global corporations must take more responsibility by changing their policies.

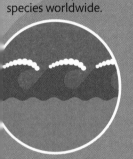

Rising sea levels cause flooding in low-lying and coastal areas, destroying natural habitats and people's homes.

Protection of oceans includes creating marine sanctuaries, conserving coral reefs, managing fishing, and preventing water pollution.

Extreme weather events, such as wildfires and heatwaves, have been linked directly to global warming.

Carbon capture is a process whereby carbon dioxide emissions from power plants are trapped, isolated, and stored, usually underground.

Reforestation involves planting trees and forests on a massive scale. This prevents soil erosion, restores wildlife habitats, improves water purity, and helps stabilize the climate.

THREATS **SOLUTIONS**

ORGANIZING GOVERNMENT

Political systems

From one-leader autocracies to democratic governments, political systems have evolved throughout history. How they have changed has depended largely on the identities of those in power and the extent to which the population has been involved in the political process.

Aristotle's forms of government

Several different political systems were tried in classical Greece, from the autocratic rule of tyrants to an early form of democracy. Having seen how these worked in practice, philosophers such as Plato and Aristotle were able to compare the pros and cons of the various systems. Aristotle noted that power is always either in the hands of a single ruler, an elite, or the people and that correct political systems serve the interests of the state, whereas those that only serve the ruler are corrupt.

IN THE INTERESTS OF THE STATE

Monarchy
A single ruler, such as a king or queen, looks after the prosperity of the state and the well-being of their subjects.

Aristocracy
The members of noble families, and property owners, act as custodians of the land and provide for the people.

Polity
The ordinary people make decisions about how the state should be governed. They do so through representatives who best understand the needs of society.

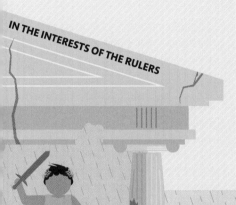

IN THE INTERESTS OF THE RULERS

THE RULE OF THE PEOPLE

In his classification of political systems, Aristotle made a subtle distinction between democracy and polity. According to his definition, democracy is government of the people, by the people, for the people, in their own interests—which may not necessarily be in the interests of the state as a whole. In Aristotle's view, a polity—a form of representative democracy regulated by a constitution—is a better form of government in that it protects the interests of both the state and its citizens. He argued that, in both cases, the rule of the many is often wiser than the rule of the few.

Tyranny
A single ruler, often one who has taken power unconstitutionally, puts their own interests before those of the state and its people.

Oligarchy
A corrupt elite exploit their position of control over the people to increase their own wealth and power.

"... **democracy is the worst form of government except all those other forms that have been tried from time to time.**"

Winston Churchill, British prime minister, in a House of Commons speech (1947)

Democracy
The ordinary people govern the state. However, the majority of people may not know what the best policies are for society as a whole (see box).

Monarchy

Originally signifying rule by an individual, nowadays monarchy is generally taken to mean rule by a member of a royal family. Monarch is a hereditary title that is generally held for life.

Family rule

Historically, monarchy has been the most common and enduring type of rule. The idea of a hereditary monarchy is an ancient one that evolved from the ruling families of early civilizations. These royal families were often considered to have a divine right to rule, an idea reinforced by symbols of power, such as a crown and throne, bestowed on the monarch in ritual coronations. Their absolute power could not be challenged except by force, either an attack by an enemy or an uprising or revolution—for example, the establishment of the Athenian democracy or the overthrow of the monarchy in the French Revolution. In such cases, the monarchy was usually abolished, and in its place a republic established. More gradual changes also occurred as social attitudes evolved, with monarchs giving up some of their powers, first to the nobility in medieval times and later to parliaments.

Modern monarchs

Even today, a significant number of countries have retained some form of hereditary monarchy. However, as the majority of states have adopted democratic models of government, the importance and

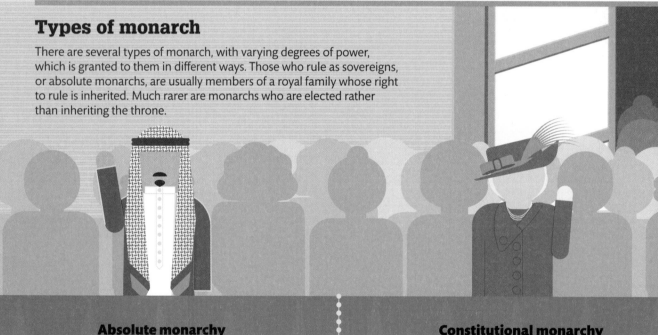

Types of monarch

There are several types of monarch, with varying degrees of power, which is granted to them in different ways. Those who rule as sovereigns, or absolute monarchs, are usually members of a royal family whose right to rule is inherited. Much rarer are monarchs who are elected rather than inheriting the throne.

Absolute monarchy

The system of a monarch as the head of government as well as the head of state has been almost completely superseded by democracies, except in a small number of conservative countries, such as Saudi Arabia.

Constitutional monarchy

Where monarchies exist today, they may still have a role in the government of the nation but are subordinate to the parliament or national assembly. This form of monarchy exists in the UK and Japan.

power of such monarchs have waned. Many nations are now republics and have replaced monarchs with an elected president as head of state; others have reduced the role of the monarch to a purely ceremonial one, in which they have little real influence in governing.

There are still a handful of absolute monarchies, in which the ruler is the sovereign power or head of government, but the majority of remaining monarchs have their power defined by the nation's constitution. The idea of a divine right to rule survives in only a few theocracies (see pp.72–73).

FEUDALISM

In medieval Europe, the duties and land ownership of the different classes were organized in what was known as the feudal system. At the top of the hierarchy, the monarch was the owner of all the land but gave some to the nobility in return for favors and taxes. They in turn made land available to knights who fought for them, and this land was then made available to the peasants, who paid for it with a proportion of the food they produced.

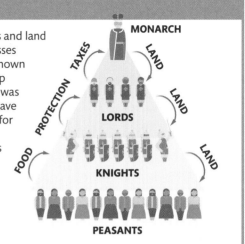

"I am the State."

Attributed to Louis XIV, king of France (1655)

Semi-constitutional monarchy

Whereas constitutional monarchs have few affairs of state, semi-constitutional monarchs are more active heads of state, with responsibilities similar to a president. For example, the monarch of Jordan holds wide executive powers.

Elective monarchy

In a few countries, the monarch is selected by an elite from a small group of candidates. The pope, chosen by the College of Cardinals as the ruler of the Roman Catholic Holy See, is a modern example of an elective monarch.

Theocracy

Religion is an important part of almost every culture, and as such, it inevitably has an influence on a nation's politics—sometimes to the extent that it dictates the way a country is governed.

Origins of theocracy

Although the word "theocracy" literally means rule by God or a god, in practice it is used to describe the government of a civil state by the leader (or leaders) of a particular religion, according to the laws prescribed by that religion.

The involvement of religious officials in government dates back to the ancient world, notably in Egypt and Syria, Tibet, and some periods of Buddhist rule in Japan and China. The idea of theocracy persisted into the Middle Ages, and even beyond. The Catholic Church wielded great political power with the pope at the head of the Holy Roman Empire, and various Islamic empires were ruled by a caliph, who was both the political and spiritual leader of Muslims around the world.

Religious rule today

There are few true theocracies in the modern world. They mainly exist in Islamic countries and include Iran, which has many religious officials in powerful governmental positions, led by a Supreme Leader who must be a respected scholar of Islamic law. Saudi Arabia is a semi-theocracy: although the monarch is not a religious official, the constitution of Saudi Arabia is the Koran and the Sunna (traditions of the Prophet Muhammad). The Roman Catholic Holy See is a notable non-Islamic example of a modern theocracy.

Many countries have an official state religion. In some cases, the head of state may also be the head of the state religion, as is the case in the United Kingdom, where the monarch is head of the Church of England. This is not considered a theocracy because the government is not seen to directly derive its powers from a divine authority.

Generally speaking, in the modern era, the trend toward liberal democracies has also meant a shift away from the involvement of religious institutions in government and toward more secular states.

THE DIVINE RIGHT OF MONARCHS

It is not only theocracies that claim God's authority to rule; until the advent of secular democracies, many royal families were assumed to have the "divine right of kings." As well as giving legitimacy to the hereditary monarchy, it was also often taken to mean that the monarch had absolute power and was accountable only to God. A similar idea existed in the dynasties of ancient China, whose kings and emperors were believed to have been granted the "mandate of heaven," or approval by the gods to rule. This mandate could be withdrawn if the monarch failed in their responsibilities as a ruler.

Divine authority

In a theocracy, the laws and even the constitution of the state are thought to be dictated by God or his agents. Government should, therefore, be in the hands of those best suited to interpret and administer these divine laws—the priests and scholars who follow God's calling.

Followers

In a theocracy, followers of the dominant religion accept the God-given authority of their rulers, respecting their judgment in interpreting and administering the law and their guidance in matters of morality.

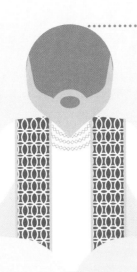

Religious leader

The leader or leaders are generally ministers of the dominant religion or scholars of the holy texts. They are considered God's representatives and are divinely guided in their actions.

Religious text

Most religions have a sacred text that contains their core beliefs, often as revealed to a prophet. The text is considered the word of God and, as such, is the infallible source of guidance for theocratic leaders.

"Religious ideas, supposedly private matters between man and god, are in practice always political ideas."

Christopher Hitchens, British-American author, *The Monarchy* (1990)

RELIGIOUS TEXT INTERPRETED

Religious law

Some laws are in the holy scriptures; others come from interpretations of the texts by theologians.

Secular assembly

In some theocracies, a secular government, secondary to the religious one, tends to the everyday running of the country.

One-party states

In times of political or economic crisis, a government may ban its opposition parties and establish an authoritarian one-party state.

A single ideology

The opposite of multi-party democracies (see pp.78–79), one-party states are generally regarded as repressive forms of government, since they are usually led by a dictator and involve the outlawing of opposition parties. Such regimes tend to be authoritarian, usually based on ideologies at the extremes of the political spectrum, such as fascism (see pp.46–47) or communism (see pp.54–55), or on fundamentalist interpretations of religious texts.

The establishment of a one-party state is often defended in terms of the need for national unity, especially in times of economic crisis or when the country is facing an external threat. Sometimes it is created by gradually eroding the opposition, as was the case with the rise of the Nazi Party in

Dangers of the one-party state

One-party states can quickly descend into totalitarian regimes. To maintain control, the government becomes increasingly authoritarian—removing all opposition and controlling more and more aspects of the lives of citizens.

STATE SECURITY
Using the protection of citizens as a pretext, the state increases the power of the police and security forces to enforce restrictive measures.

PARTY ALLEGIANCE
Citizens are expected to show loyalty to the state and its leader as well as patriotic allegiance to the country.

Germany. However, occasionally the opposition is swiftly silenced—for example, after a revolution or coup d'état.

Suppressing dissent

To maintain its hold on power, the ruling party has to continually suppress dissent. As well as outlawing opposition parties, it may introduce laws to prevent individuals from criticizing the state. It may also use state institutions, such as the police, the armed forces, the media, and schools, to exercise increasing control over its citizens.

If the state's ideology is imposed in an increasingly authoritarian way, affecting every aspect of citizens' public and private lives, it becomes regarded as totalitarian. Totalitarianism, the most extreme form of one-party system, gained strength during the 20th century with the rise of Nazism, fascism, communism, and religious fundamentalism.

CASE STUDY

Cuba

In 1959, during the Cuban Revolution, the corrupt regime of Fulgencio Batista was overthrown and replaced by a communist government led by Fidel Castro. Since the 1960s, Cuba has been a one-party state, and no opposition to the ruling Communist Party of Cuba has been allowed. Although Cuba's regime is widely regarded as repressive, the country is renowned for having developed one of the world's most efficient health care systems.

> "The essence of totalitarianism... is to make functionaries out of men."

Hannah Arendt, German-Jewish political philosopher, *Eichmann in Jerusalem* (1963)

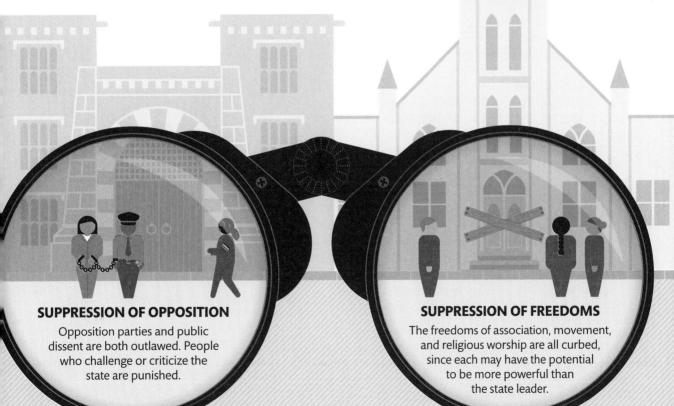

SUPPRESSION OF OPPOSITION

Opposition parties and public dissent are both outlawed. People who challenge or criticize the state are punished.

SUPPRESSION OF FREEDOMS

The freedoms of association, movement, and religious worship are all curbed, since each may have the potential to be more powerful than the state leader.

Dictatorship

A dictatorship is an authoritarian regime in which a single individual wields absolute power over the state and does not need the consent of the citizens.

Gaining power

History is full of examples of autocratic leaders assuming control over states. However, it is only in modern times that the term "dictator" has become unambiguously negative. In the 20th century, it became associated with the leaders of brutal totalitarian regimes (see pp.46–47), such as Nazi Germany, Francoist Spain, the Soviet Union, and Maoist China. While dictators may oversee totalitarian regimes, dictatorships are distinguished by being led by a single powerful leader or small group; totalitarianism is defined by the repressive control the state extends to all aspects of citizens' lives.

Although many dictators seize power in times of crisis, some, such as Adolf Hitler, are legitimately elected into office, only to then extend their powers to take full control of the state. However, whichever way they come to power, dictators invariably need the support of the military and intelligence services.

Staying in power

After a military coup, a high-ranking military officer usually becomes leader. When a civilian takes charge, they typically assume the rank of general to gain control of the armed forces. Some modern dictators may hand back power once a period of crisis is over, but many remain for life. Since the leader cannot be removed through political means, they can only be forced out—by public protest or military coup.

Absolute control

In order to maintain absolute power, dictators have to control both the people and the state. As head of state, they become the sole authority for their state's legal and political decisions. Although dictatorships may begin as a declared interim measure, some leaders never step down again. They take control of the police, the military, and the intelligence services, which enables them to silence dissent, constrain the media, and broadcast state propaganda.

Silence dissent
With the support of the police and the security services, dictators silence opposition in order to maintain their position of power.

Control public institutions
As well as ensuring the support of the police and the military, dictators take control of public institutions, such as universities and local government offices.

Overrule processes

During a state of emergency, a ruler can override democratic process, but only as an interim measure; a dictator may extend this period indefinitely.

Constrain the media

Dictators can stifle dissent, shut down independent newspapers and channels, and broadcast their own propaganda.

Become executive branch

As absolute ruler, a dictator becomes both head of government and head of state. As such, they effectively become the executive branch of government. For this reason, they often adopt the title of president.

Oversee laws

As head of government, dictators oversee the legislature and maintain a tight control of the judiciary (the courts that administer the law).

CASE STUDY

Josip Broz Tito

After commanding the Yugoslav Partisans during World War II, Josip Tito (1892–1980) helped found the Socialist Federal Republic of Yugoslavia in 1945. He served as the country's prime minster, and later president, from 1945 until his death in 1980. Although his rule was autocratic, Tito was regarded as a benign dictator—even standing up to Joseph Stalin of the USSR. He unified the nations that made up the Federal Republic and gained considerable respect.

Multi-party democracy

Democracy depends on citizens being able to cast their votes in elections. However, not all voting systems are the same, and some are considered to be more democratic than others.

The choice of the electorate

Unlike one-party states (see pp.74–75), two- or multi-party states have two or more political parties that the public can vote for in elections. In two-party states, such as the US, two political parties dominate the political landscape, and almost all the elected officials are members of those camps. However, this does not mean that other parties are banned. In the US, for example, although the Democratic and Republican parties dominate, since its founding in 1971, the Libertarian Party (see pp.42–43) has gained influence, and some of its members have been elected to local government office.

Two-party political systems are often called first-past-the-post (FPTP) systems because they allow only one party to win an election, leaving the other party to

Ruling parties

Defenders of the first-past-the-post system argue that it leads to strong governments that generally stand united and are able to draft legislation swiftly. They also claim that FPTP creates a strong opposition party that is united in its criticisms of the government. Defenders of proportional representation argue that FPTP can leave many voters disenfranchised or unrepresented by the government in power. They also claim that such voters may also disagree with the policies of the opposition party, meaning that they are effectively alienated by the entire political system.

Ruling and opposition parties
With often only a small majority, a single political party forms the entire government. Its only opposition is the second party, which will stay in opposition unless it defeats the government in a general election.

Rival parties
During general elections, the two main parties present their policies to the public. The party that receives the greatest number of votes either stays in power or replaces the existing government.

Broad base appeal
Voters have a range of political views, many of which may not be represented by the two main parties. During elections, they vote for the party that best represents their interests.

TWO-PARTY SYSTEM

POLITICAL PARTIES

VOTERS AND THEIR POLITICAL BELIEFS

form the opposition. However, this term is also used to describe multi-party systems of the kind found in the UK and India. In the UK, for example, anyone can form a political party and run for election, but if they fail to win a seat in parliament, their party is not represented in government. A party can even have multiple candidates and collectively receive millions of votes but still fail to win a parliamentary seat. To avoid this scenario, many countries have a system known as proportional representation (PR).

A fairer system

Proportional representation (see pp.110–11) is based on the idea that an elected parliament should not only represent the two dominant political parties. Instead, it should represent all the major parties, and the number of elected officials should be proportional to the share of the vote that each party receives. For example, if a party receives a quarter of the vote, then its representatives should also receive a quarter of the seats in parliament.

> "So two cheers for democracy: one because it admits variety and two because it permits criticism."
>
> E. M. Forster, British writer, *What I Believe* (1938)

MULTI-PARTY SYSTEM

Coalition parties
The government is a coalition of politicians who represent a number of political parties. It is essentially a group of parties that work together to find solutions to political issues.

POLITICAL PARTIES

Multiple parties
Multiple parties contest the elections. The most popular parties form the next government. Each takes a share of the seats that is proportional to the share of the votes that the party won.

VOTERS AND THEIR POLITICAL BELIEFS

Diverse interests
Voters have a range of views, many of which are represented by political parties. The electorate votes for these parties with the knowledge that their concerns will be addressed by the government.

RANKED-CHOICE VOTING

Another way of establishing a winner in multi-party systems is to use ranked-choice voting (RCV). From the candidates on the polling form, voters are asked to rank either all or a specified number (perhaps a top three) in order of preference. Usually, if a candidate receives more than half of the first-choice votes, that candidate wins. However, if there is no majority winner, the candidate with the fewest votes is eliminated, and voters who picked that candidate as their number-one choice have their votes for their second-place choice counted. Supporters of RCV argue that it ensures that the winner has the approval of the majority of voters. It also avoids the need for second polls. RCV is used in national and state elections in Australia, Malta, and Slovenia.

Federalism

Many countries have two main levels of government: the central, or federal, government and the regional, or state, government. This dual form of government is known as federalism.

Two tiers of government

Federalism is a form of government that recognizes that, although a country may require a strong central government that legislates on matters of national interest, it may also require regional, or state, authorities that can legislate on regional issues. In the US, for example, it is illegal to counterfeit money under federal law, and doing so is a crime in all 50 US states. However, although all US citizens have the right to bear firearms, whether they can do so openly varies from state to state. Likewise, when Switzerland became a federal state in 1848, its 26 regions, or cantons, had to disband their standing armies, but each retained considerable autonomy, which served to strengthen the country as a whole.

In general, as well as legislating on domestic issues, federal governments have the power to regulate national and international trade, manage foreign affairs, and maintain their countries' armed forces. On the other hand, regional governments are free to regulate the industries that operate within their states, set up local government authorities, and pass laws that address specific local concerns.

Division of powers

According to the United Nations' definition of federalism, a federal government must be responsible for national security and foreign policy in order for it to be considered a sovereign state. The exact powers of the component states are determined by the constitution of the country.

Public services

Citizens of federations usually pay a federal tax as well as a state tax. The state tax contributes to maintaining vital public services, such as police forces, schools, and hospitals.

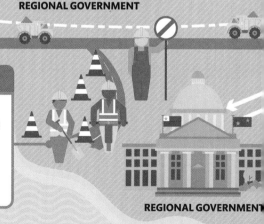

REGIONAL GOVERNMENT

DEVOLUTION

Devolution is a form of federalism, but one that differs in significant ways. For example, in the UK, the countries of Scotland, Wales, and Northern Ireland each have semi-independent governments; in Denmark, the Faroe Islands and Greenland are devolved regions. However, unlike federal states, these devolved governments can have their powers withdrawn by the central government, which is where power ultimately resides.

Infrastructure

State governments are responsible for building public roads and bridges. However, interstate highways and airports may be subsidized by the federal government.

REGIONAL GOVERNMENT

FEDERAL GOVERNMENT RESPONSIBILITIES

FOREIGN POLICY

The federal government has three key responsibilities. Firstly, it controls the state's foreign policy, which determines the nature of its relationships with other countries.

DEFENSE

Secondly, it maintains the state's military forces and determines when the country will go to war. Thirdly, it has control over the state's national and international economic policies.

ECONOMIC POLICY

This includes the power to raise and regulate taxes, which contribute to paying for the country's national public services, and to conduct international trade.

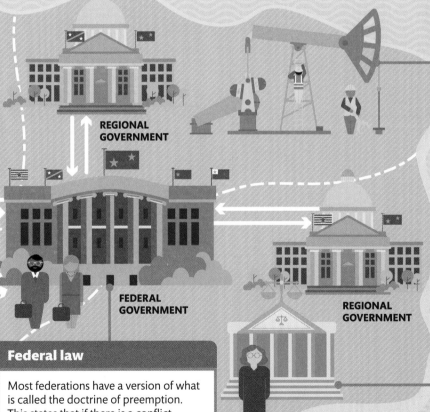

REGIONAL GOVERNMENT

FEDERAL GOVERNMENT

REGIONAL GOVERNMENT

Natural resources

The federal government is usually the owner of all of a country's natural resources. However, the state that exploits these resources usually receives most of the revenue from them.

Legal systems

Component states are responsible for their own court systems, which adjudicate on matters of state law. They also host federal courts, which deal with cases concerning federal law.

Federal law

Most federations have a version of what is called the doctrine of preemption. This states that if there is a conflict between a federal law and a state law, the federal law takes precedence.

Political institutions

Political institutions are the organizations that govern political behavior in a country or state. They are particularly important because they place limits on the power of governments and politicians. For example, they include electoral rules that establish how governments are elected and replaced. They also include constitutional rules that determine the powers and responsibilities of different parts of government in relation to establishing the law.

Separation of powers

A key issue for democracies is ensuring that those elected to office do not abuse their power. One of the ways this is achieved is through establishing political institutions that distribute power to different parts of government. The French philosopher Baron de Montesquieu (1689–1755) promoted the idea of "tripartite" systems, with three branches of government—executive, legislative, and judicial—providing checks on each other.

Legislative branch

The legislative branch is responsible for making the law in a country. In democracies, the legislature usually takes the form of an assembly—such as Congress in the US or parliament in the UK—in which elected representatives meet to discuss and decide on legislation.

Executive branch

The executive branch is responsible for implementing and administering the laws made by the legislature. In presidential systems, the executive branch is independent of the legislative branch; in parliamentary systems, there is some overlap between the two branches.

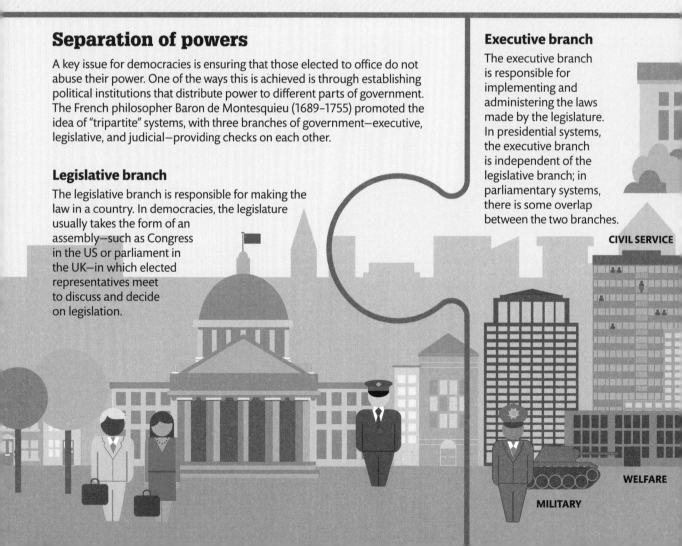

CIVIL SERVICE

MILITARY

WELFARE

CONSTITUTIONS

Constitutions are the legal foundation for government in virtually every country around the world. They organize and regulate state power. Constitutions broadly refer to a set of fundamental principles and more specific provisions to which governments and laws must conform.

These principles establish how a country should be governed and how laws are made. They can also include the fundamental rights of citizens. Most countries have a written constitution. However, notable exceptions are New Zealand and the UK, which have a collection of key legislation, judicial decisions, and treaties that are collectively referred to as their constitutions.

"When the **legislative and executive powers are united in the same person, or in the same body of magistrates, there can be no liberty.**"

Montesquieu, *The Spirit of the Laws* (1748)

Judicial branch

The judicial branch interprets and applies the laws made by the legislature and upheld by the executive branch. It includes the systems of courts and judges in a country that rule on legal disputes between the state and individuals. The judiciary ensures that government actions are in accordance with the law and that laws are consistent with the constitution.

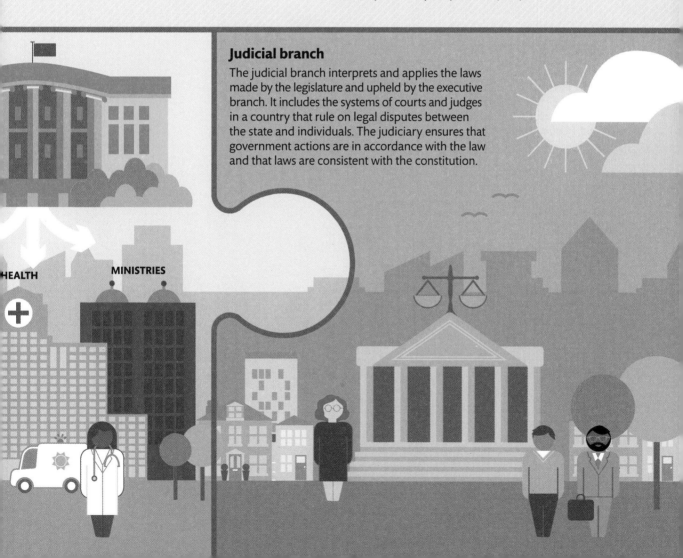

HEALTH

MINISTRIES

Executive branch

The executive is the branch of government that is responsible for ensuring that laws and policies are carried out. It includes a country's key political leaders, such as the president or prime minister.

Governing the country

When people talk about the government of a country, they are typically referring to the executive branch of government. The executive branch is responsible for enforcing the law and for the daily administration of the country. This includes planning and implementing government policy across different areas, such as the economy, health, and education, and providing public services. It does all this through various agencies and departments.

The head of the executive (or head of government) is the prime minister in parliamentary systems and the president in presidential systems. These people are generally considered to be the leader of the country.

A separation of powers exists to ensure those in office do not abuse their power. Although the legislative branch is responsible for making laws, the executive

Executive systems

The way the executive branch functions, particularly in terms of its powers and relationship to the legislative branch, depends on the type of governing system. Most democracies have either parliamentary or presidential systems, but some have a hybrid system.

The prime minister is the head of the executive branch in parliamentary systems and is also a member of the legislative branch.

The cabinet consists of legislature members who are selected by the prime minister to lead key ministries.

The legislative and executive branches overlap. The executive is accountable to the legislature.

PARLIAMENTARY SYSTEMS

PRIME MINISTER

CABINET

LEGISLATORS

The head of state in parliamentary systems is typically not the head of government but a constitutional monarch or ceremonial president.

When voting, citizens elect legislators but do not directly elect the prime minister. The party with the most parliamentary seats selects the prime minister from the legislature.

BALLOT BOX

branch has the power to introduce some types of law by executive decree or executive order.

Members of the executive

As well as the head of the executive, other members include the leaders of government departments or ministries. The highest ranking of these are members of the cabinet, who offer advice and help decide on key policies. The branch also includes the head of state—the highest representative of the country.

DUTIES OF THE EXECUTIVE BRANCH

In order to ensure the smooth running of the country on a daily basis, the executive branch of the government has a variety of responsibilities.

❯ **Enforcing the law** via government departments and a police force

❯ **Implementing policies** across different areas, such as health, education, and the economy

❯ **Overseeing national security**, with responsibility for the military and intelligence services

❯ **Establishing foreign policy**, including responsibilities such as the signing of international treaties, or agreements, with other countries

❯ **Nominating candidates** for major appointments, including members of the judiciary and the civil service

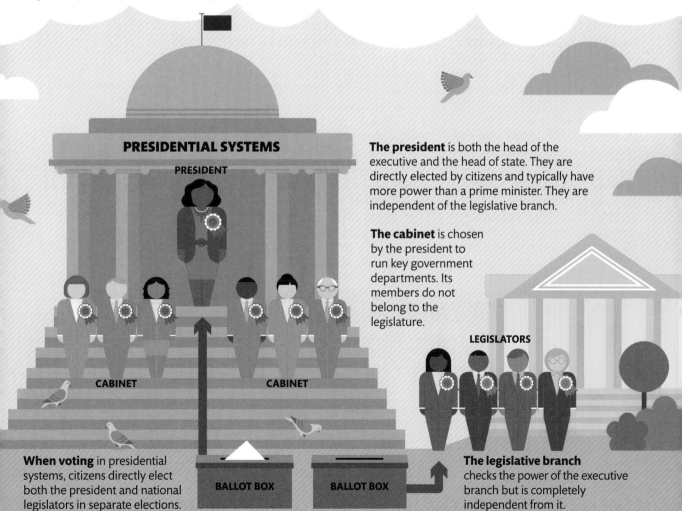

PRESIDENTIAL SYSTEMS

PRESIDENT

CABINET

CABINET

LEGISLATORS

The president is both the head of the executive and the head of state. They are directly elected by citizens and typically have more power than a prime minister. They are independent of the legislative branch.

The cabinet is chosen by the president to run key government departments. Its members do not belong to the legislature.

When voting in presidential systems, citizens directly elect both the president and national legislators in separate elections.

BALLOT BOX

BALLOT BOX

The legislative branch checks the power of the executive branch but is completely independent from it.

Legislative branch

The legislative branch is responsible for making laws in a country. Legislatures in democratic systems are assemblies in which elected representatives gather to deliberate and decide on laws.

The origins of legislatures

Throughout history, assemblies in which people gather to debate and agree on new laws have been a key feature of societies with some degree of self-government (unlike those ruled by monarchs with absolute power). This type of assembly was fundamental to ancient Athenian democracy and existed in countries such as India in the 6th–4th centuries BCE and Persia (present-day Iran) in the 4th century BCE. By 900 CE, the Vikings in the Nordic countries had created local assemblies to decide on new laws. These assemblies and those emerging in other parts of Europe evolved into modern legislatures.

How legislatures work

In modern democracies, most legislative branches consist of representatives who are elected by citizens living in a particular geographic area, or constituency.

These legislators represent the interests of their constituents. Citizens often decide which legislative candidate to vote for based on the political party to which the candidate belongs. This means that parties—representing political ideologies or specific classes—have a strong influence on the laws made by legislatures.

A key function of the legislature is deliberation, whereby legislators discuss and debate proposed laws. This process may occur across the legislature or through committees if legislators are focusing on specific policy areas. Following this deliberation and any amendments, the legislature will usually vote on the proposed law.

The legislature has the power to collect taxes, declare war, and authorize treaties and expenditure. Legislators can also hold the executive to account through a system of checks and balances.

2. Deliberation and debate
Legislators discuss the proposed law, considering its merits and limitations. This can take place in the legislature as a whole or in specific committees.

UNICAMERAL OR BICAMERAL

Legislatures can be unicameral or bicameral. In unicameral systems, the legislature debates and votes on laws as a single unit. In bicameral systems, legislatures consist of upper and lower chambers (or houses), with legislation having to pass through both of these political structures.

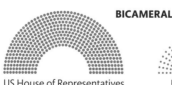

UNICAMERAL

Iceland's Althing
63 seats

BICAMERAL

US House of Representatives
435 seats

US Senate
100 seats

1. Bill introduced
The first stage is when either the government or a member of the legislature drafts a proposed law and presents it to the legislature.

5. Enactment
The executive (in presidential systems) or the head of state gives the final approval for the proposed ill, enabling it to be passed into law.

4. Voting
After further debate, the legislature holds a vote on whether to pass or reject the bill. In bicameral systems, both upper and lower chambers vote on the bill.

3. Amendments
A group of legislators, usually in a specific committee, then consider more closely how the law will work in practice and may make changes to improve it.

> "... equality... means the right to participate in the making of the laws by which one is governed..."
>
> Nelson Mandela, South African president, court statement (1962)

How laws are made

The exact process by which the legislative branch makes laws varies across countries and political systems. The process is not always linear—particularly in bicameral systems, in which proposed legislation can pass back and forth between the two chambers. However, the process typically consists of several stages, which include the introduction of a bill (proposal for a law), deliberation and debate, amendments, voting, and the enactment of the law.

Judicial branch

The judicial branch is responsible for interpreting, defending, and applying the law. Its systems of courts and judges make decisions on legal disagreements between the state and individuals.

The court system

The judicial branch is the court system in a country that interprets and applies the law, and helps in the resolution of disputes. The responsibilities of the judiciary are set out in a nation's constitution.

An independent judiciary ensures that government actions operate in accordance with the rule of law. Additionally, it settles legal disputes between the state and individuals, playing a key role in protecting the rights of people.

The judicial branch functions through the court system, in which legal cases are brought before the court and presided over by judges. The court system has a hierarchical structure that includes local-level courts (such as magistrates or county courts) extending up to the highest court in the country, known as a supreme court, apex court, or court of last resort. These high-level courts typically function as courts of appeal, hearing appeals against decisions made by lower courts in the system. In many countries, high-level courts also determine the validity of laws based on whether they are consistent with the constitution.

Civil or common law

Countries' legal systems follow the civil law or the common law, and sometimes a combination of the two. Civil law emphasizes the codification of the law (arranging it in a system); common law is based on judicial precedents (earlier rulings by judges).

Judges lead
Legal practitioners, such as lawyers, advise clients and represent their interests, but it is judges who take the lead by bringing charges and examining witnesses.

Civil law
Judges have less influence on how the law is interpreted. Instead, their job is to establish the facts of a case and apply resolutions found in written statutes and legal codes. Countries that have a civil law system include Germany, China, and Spain.

Interpreting the law

While the judicial branch is not responsible for making laws, the ways in which it interprets the law can have significant implications for how the law is applied in a country. This partly depends on the type of legal system in that country and whether this is based on common law or civil law.

Unlike the legislative and executive branches of government, members of the judicial branch are typically not elected by citizens; instead, they are individuals with legal training and qualifications.

Given their independence from the executive and legislative branches, members of the judicial branch are required to interpret the law with justice in mind and to ignore any political bias or electoral matters.

In some countries, such as the US, members of the judicial branch are appointed by the executive and confirmed by the legislative branch. By contrast, in the UK in 2005, reforms were introduced that meant judges were no longer selected by the Lord Chancellor—a member of the executive—but by an independent commission.

CASE STUDY

Brown vs. Board of Education

The landmark 1954 US Supreme Court case *Brown vs. Board of Education of Topeka* demonstrates how judicial rulings can bring about fundamental change to the systems operating within a country.

Before the case in Kansas was brought, education and other services were segregated in the US. Black children could not attend the same schools as their white peers. The case was challenged in court, advancing to the US Supreme Court, which ruled that segregation was unconstitutional because it deprived Black children of equal opportunities. The ruling ended segregation in public schools—and was an important catalyst for the civil rights movement and racial equality in the country.

PRECEDENTS

Common law
Judges take an active role in shaping the law, as the decisions they make are used as precedents—examples or analogies—for future judges to follow. Countries that have a common law system include the UK, the US, and Australia.

Judges referee
Legal practitioners make presentations and examine witnesses, trying to persuade the court of points of law and fact. The proceedings are refereed by an impartial judge.

Civil service

The civil service helps with the day-to-day functioning of the state by delivering public services and supporting the government in the design, development, and implementation of policies.

From policies to practice

The civil service, or bureaucracy, refers to the many government officials who provide services to the public and help draw up and implement government policies. Unlike politicians in a democratic system, civil servants are not elected. Instead, they are recruited based on merit, and during their time in office, they may see several changes of government.

The origins of a meritocratic civil service can be traced back to the administrative system of government in imperial China around 207 BCE. At this time, anyone could become a civil servant, providing they passed examinations that tested candidates' knowledge of Confucian philosophy and other subjects, such as mathematics. The modern civil service developed in Britain in the 19th century. Inspired by the Chinese tests, reforms were introduced to establish a meritocratic civil service that could manage Britain's growing empire.

The ideal bureaucracy

Historically, bureaucracies have not been based on merit. Instead, political parties that came to power would reward supporters and family with civil service jobs. This meant civil servants often lacked the

Policy making in the civil service

Civil servants play an essential role in the policy-making process. They answer to the government and support government ministers, such as the Minister of Education, in the design and implementation of policies— for example, trying to increase the number of women graduating with a science degree.

2. Assessing policy methods
Civil servants in the Ministry of Education consider different ways to achieve the policy objective and what each method would entail.

1. Deciding policy objective
The Minister of Education decides on a policy objective—for example, to increase the number of women graduating from university with a science degree.

"… **an institutional method for** applying general rules **to** specific cases."

Max Weber on bureaucracy, *Economy and Society* (1922)

competence or experience to deliver effective policies. It also fueled corruption, with citizens forced to pay bribes to civil servants in order to access public services.

According to the German sociologist Max Weber (1864–1920), in addition to meritocratic recruitment, an ideal bureaucracy should have other key characteristics, such as being rule-based and hierarchical. In practice, most civil services around the world do not possess all of these traits. In many countries, such as the US, Germany, and Iraq, senior civil servants are politically appointed.

5. Implementing policy
Civil servants working across different levels of public administration ensure that the policy is put into practice and then assess its effectiveness.

4. Selecting policy
The Minister of Education decides on the best policy option. In some countries, the executive branch also needs to approve the policy.

3. Exploring policy options
The civil servants propose different policy options to the Minister of Education, along with the costs and benefits of each of those options.

WEBER'S SIX CHARACTERISTICS

According to Weber, there are six qualities that a bureaucracy should have:

> **A hierarchical management structure** that ensures accountability at every level

> **A clear division of labor**, where jobs are broken down into simple and well-defined tasks

> **A formal and merit-based recruitment process** that ensures civil servants are selected according to their technical skills and competencies

> **Career advancement** that is based on achievement, experience, and technical qualifications (not personal favors or relationships)

> **Formal rules and regulations** whereby civil servants know exactly what is expected of them

> **An impersonal environment** in which all employees are treated equally (to avoid nepotism or favoritism)

Government departments

A government is divided up into departments or ministries organized according to their importance. Each department oversees a specific aspect of government and is responsible for implementing policy.

Policy to practice

The executive branch is the area of government that deals with the daily running of the state. It is organized into departments, each of which is responsible for different sectors and areas of policy. The departments use different names, depending on the country's political system. In most parliamentary systems, they are called ministries, but in presidential systems, they may be known as executive departments, bureaus, or secretariats. Each department is made up of civil servants and is led by a politician (the minister or secretary) who is part of the executive. The key departments are led by senior politicians who form the cabinet office. The departmental minister

Key departments

The specific executive departments or ministries that are considered the most important in a country can vary, depending on the types of policy issues that the country faces. However, across most countries, these core departments tend to have similar purposes, focusing on the key government responsibilities and policy areas.

Highest office

The office of either the prime minister or the president sets and delivers the government's overall strategy and policy priorities and will relay those policies to the public.

Treasury

Also called the finance ministry, the treasury oversees economic and finance policy. Its job includes making public-spending decisions, setting economic policy, and achieving economic growth for the nation.

Department of Health

Overseeing government policy on health and social care, this office targets many issues, from ensuring access to basic healthcare to pandemic response. A core aim is to improve domestic and global public health.

Ministry of Defense

The defense policies of a country are set by this department. It is also responsible for issues relating to international peace and security, and it oversees the day-to-day running of the military.

Foreign Office

This office is responsible for a country's foreign policy. It also protects and promotes national interests globally, such as national security, trade and investment, global agreements, and help for citizens abroad.

establishes the core priorities in collaboration with the president or prime minister's office. It is the job of the civil servants to come up with different policy options, secure their minister's support, and then implement those policies.

Departmental dynamics

While each department is typically responsible for a specific policy area, such as education or business, issues that arise can span different areas. For example, if there are not enough qualified engineers in a country, there is an overlap between business and education. Therefore, departments will often need to work together to devise and implement effective policies. Coordination between departments is usually overseen by the prime minister's or president's office.

Governments have annual fixed budgets, so there is competition for resources across departments. The treasury allocates government resources, and each department is likely to argue why they need more money than their counterparts.

OTHER TYPES OF DEPARTMENTS

There are many different sectors within government, such as non-ministerial departments, which are headed by senior civil servants and have a regulatory or inspection function. There are also executive agencies that deliver services rather than set policy and public bodies that provide expert advice on specific policy areas.

Cabinet office

This consists of the heads of all the key departments. The cabinet supports and advises the prime minister's or the president's office to ensure the effective running of the government.

> **"The care of human life and happiness... is the first and only... object of good government."**
>
> Thomas Jefferson, former US president, addressing citizens of Maryland, US (1809)

Home Office

All aspects of internal security, law and order, and immigration are overseen by this office. It is responsible for specific areas, such as the police, border control, and granting identity documents.

Ministry of Trade

A country's industry, trade, and commerce are overseen by this ministry. Its role includes responsibility for setting trade agreements with other countries as well as promoting foreign investment and trade.

Department of Agriculture

This office sets the laws and policies linked to farming in a country. It deals with forestry, food, rural development, and fisheries. This department is also responsible for protecting a nation's natural resources.

Department of Education

Heading up a country's education policy, this office deals with early pre-school education and schools, as well as higher and further education policy. It can also take responsibility for child protection.

Treasuries and economic policy

The treasury, or finance ministry, is one of the most important government departments. It oversees economic policy, which means it is responsible for public finances, public spending, and financial regulation.

Running the economy

The treasury is responsible for financial and economic policy. This includes taking care of public finances, both in terms of how the government raises funds and how it spends them. The treasury is also responsible for the smooth running of the economy. This can include promoting economic growth and high employment as well as keeping inflation low, reducing poverty, and lowering levels of inequality.

In many countries, the treasury can raise taxes so that the government has more money to spend. It may also change the government's taxation policy in order to influence other economic conditions. For example, it may reduce taxes to encourage people to spend more money, with the aim of increasing economic growth. This use of government spending and taxation to influence economic conditions is known as fiscal policy. In the US, the treasury cannot raise or lower taxes and can only advise the government on fiscal policy.

Another way in which a government may try to influence economic conditions is by changing the interest rate or controlling how much money is in circulation. Known as monetary policy, these measures are often the responsibility of the central bank rather than the treasury. The treasury is usually overseen by a senior politician, who is referred to as the treasurer, the secretary of the treasury, the finance minister, or the chancellor of the exchequer.

Government income and expenditure

The government generates revenue and spends its money in various ways. How it does so is influenced by its political ideology, and by the election pledges made by the political party. Left-wing governments tend to increase public spending and favor high, progressive taxation; right-wing governments tend to keep both public spending and taxation low.

✓ NEED TO KNOW

> **Inflation** refers to the general rise in prices in an economy over time.
> **An interest rate** is the percentage charged on the amount of money borrowed or paid on the amount of money saved.
> **A central bank** manages a country's currency and monetary policy and oversees its commercial banking system.
> **Progressive taxation** is a system in which the tax rate increases as the amount of taxable income increases.

Other expenditures
Governments spend money on a range of other things, including domestic policy priorities, debt repayment, and foreign aid.

Public order and safety
Public order and safety expenses range from training police officers to funding the court system.

Defense
Spending on defense includes employing and training soldiers and purchasing high-tech weapons systems.

Taxes
The main method of raising funds is through taxation, whereby citizens pay money to the government. There are various forms of taxation, such as income tax, property tax, and sales tax.

Printing more money
Governments sometimes generate income by printing more money. To do this, the central bank transfers money to the government by purchasing bonds.

Borrowing
Governments can borrow money by issuing bonds to banks and investors, promising repayment with interest. Governments also borrow from international financial institutions.

Government income

Other sources of income
Countries may generate revenue from customs duties (see pp.170–71) or by investing in financial assets. Other, low-income countries may receive funds in the form of foreign aid (see pp.190–91).

SOEs
Some governments own corporations, known as state-owned enterprises (SOEs), and make money from the profits that they generate. Governments can also raise funds by selling SOEs.

Expenditure

Industry and agriculture
Governments support their economies by investing in industry and providing support to farmers.

Housing
Governments often provide funds for building public housing and ensuring that people have access to accommodation.

Education
Educational spending includes employing teachers, building schools, and providing loans for students to attend college.

Transport
Government spending often helps ensure that trains, buses, and subway systems operate efficiently.

Health
Spending on health includes providing emergency services, training nurses and doctors, and equipping hospitals.

Social protection
Many countries have social safety nets, whereby the government helps its citizens meet their basic needs.

Welfare

Welfare refers to support that governments provide to help citizens meet their basic needs. Welfare programs take different forms and cover a variety of issues, including healthcare, housing, and pensions.

What is welfare?

People are often unable to meet their basic needs because they lack sufficient income, live in deprived areas, or are unable to work due to a disability. In many countries around the world, governments provide some form of support to ensure that everybody achieves a minimum standard of living. This is referred to as welfare.

Welfare support is provided in many ways. There are examples of societies throughout history offering some form of welfare, but most welfare provision emerged during the late 19th century in Europe and expanded rapidly after World War II.

Welfare or not?

The extent to which governments should provide welfare is debated in most societies—often along ideological lines. Arguments in support of welfare are associated with those on the political left. These arguments focus on the moral duty of the state to ensure citizens achieve a minimum standard of living and emphasize equality of opportunity for all. Some also highlight the gains for society overall. For example, children who receive adequate food and clothing are likely to do better in school and go on to contribute more to society as an adult.

Arguments against welfare are usually associated with the political right. They focus on the high cost of welfare to the state, which is then largely passed on to ordinary taxpaying citizens. Critics of welfare also claim that it can disincentivize people from finding work and generally lead to inefficiencies in the economy.

Income support
Funds given to people on a low income to help them meet their basic needs

Child benefit
Financial support for parents or guardians who are responsible for bringing up a child

THE WELFARE STATE

The welfare state is a form of government in which the state protects and promotes the economic and social well-being of its citizens. It is based on the belief that it is a public responsibility to ensure that everybody can meet their basic needs. Chancellor Otto von Bismark (1815–98) created the first welfare state in Germany in the 1880s. The idea spread across Western Europe and the US during the early 20th century.

Types of welfare

Welfare programs take a wide variety of forms, such as offering financial support or housing at a reduced cost. They target different groups, such as parents or the elderly, and cover a range of issues, including employment, childcare, and disability.

"The object of the government is the welfare of the people."

Theodore Roosevelt, former US president, *The New Nationalism* (1910)

Job seeker's allowance
Money given to unemployed people looking for work to help them meet minimum living standards

Caregiver's allowance
Financial support for those caring for a person with a disability or illness

Disability living allowance
Money provided to people with a disability to help them meet their basic needs

Attendance allowance
Financial help for people with disabilities or illnesses who require a caregiver

Tax credits
Financial support for working people in specific circumstances that mean they need extra help

Housing benefit
Financial help to pay rent for people who are unemployed, on low incomes, or claiming other benefits

Pension credits
Extra money provided to retirees to help them meet their basic needs

Pension
A fund that people pay into during their working lives and from which they can withdraw money after they retire

Winter fuel allowance
Support provided to elderly people to help cover the cost of heating their homes

Conditional cash transfer
Financial help for those in poverty in return for fulfilling a requirement, such as enrolling a child in school

Maternity pay
Funds paid to women who are pregnant or have recently had children and are not working

The military

Collectively known as the armed forces, a nation's military is responsible for its defense against external threats or internal conflict. In most countries, the military is overseen by the executive.

The role of the military

According to German sociologist Max Weber, the most defining characteristic of the state is the monopoly on legitimate use of violence. The military is the state institution that typically holds this exclusive right. Historically, as people have organized into distinct political entities, some gained the role of protecting others from external threats by using force.

In most countries, the armed forces consist of various branches, including the army, the navy, and the air force. Governments often spend vast sums of money ensuring that their military is large enough to defend the nation—and is highly trained and well equipped with advanced weapons technology. The size of a country's military is also often seen as an indicator of its power. In some countries, adults are conscripted into military service.

Throughout history, the military has been used not only to invade and conquer other lands but also to defend and secure its country. However, when nations strengthen their militaries for security purposes, surrounding countries can feel threatened, and the situation may trigger a conflict. This is known as the security dilemma. As a result, there has been much emphasis in global politics on disarmament— in particular, nuclear disarmament.

Other functions

The military has other roles and responsibilities. The special training soldiers receive and their experience with working in crisis situations have meant they are often deployed in emergency responses. For example, in nations such as the UK, the army played a vital role in responding to the COVID-19 pandemic by helping

local authorities test for the virus, set up mass vaccination sites, and deliver vaccines. Governments may also send their forces to help during humanitarian crises at home and abroad.

COUNTRIES WITH HIGHEST MILITARY SPENDING

In 2020, the US ranked the highest in the world in terms of military spending, amounting to more than 3 percent of its GDP (gross domestic product).

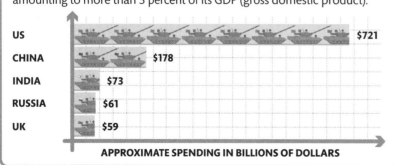

US	$721
CHINA	$178
INDIA	$73
RUSSIA	$61
UK	$59

APPROXIMATE SPENDING IN BILLIONS OF DOLLARS

Control of the military

A central issue for nearly all countries is the relationship between the civilian government (specifically, the executive) and the military. The exact nature of this relationship is usually set out in a country's constitution. In most cases, the executive has control over the military, with the military being accountable to the executive. In some contexts, however, the relationship between the two may be different.

State control of military

In most democracies, governments have control over the military. In the US, for example, the president is referred to as the commander-in-chief, as they have authority over the military.

Military as a rival power

In some nations, such as Bolivia, the military represents a rival source of power to the civilian government. Key duties may be split between the executive and military, which can cause political tensions.

Military rule

Some countries, such as Sudan and Myanmar, are ruled by the military, with no civilian government. Citizens have little say in the politics of such military dictatorships.

No military

Some countries do not have a military. In the cases of Costa Rica and Grenada, for example, the standing army was abolished due to the threat of coups, with military spending diverted to such areas as education.

$1.981tn

was spent globally on the military in 2020.

Stockholm International Peace Research Institute (2021)

Local government

The function of local government is to provide key services to local residents and businesses. These may include social care, schools, housing, waste collection, and business support.

Everyday local politics

Discussions about politics often focus on national issues, but it is typically local government that people engage with on a daily basis. This is because local authorities provide a range of key services to residents and businesses. The term "local government" broadly refers to the lowest levels of public administration, which operate in specific geographic localities, in contrast to "central government," which usually refers to the national—or state—government.

The specific form of local government that people engage with depends on where they live. For example, people living in a city may have a different type of local authority, with distinct responsibilities, than people living in a small village in the same country. Local governments around the world include local councils, county councils, municipalities, parishes, and communes, among many others. Furthermore, depending on where a person lives, there may be a single tier of local government that is responsible for providing key services or two tiers of government, with responsibilities split between them.

In democratic systems, citizens typically elect the people serving on local councils in local elections. Candidates who run for election may be members of national political parties or independents who have chosen to run on specific local issues of importance. Local authorities also include unelected staff who are hired to focus on local priorities.

Responsibilities of local government

Local governments are responsible for managing the resources of local communities. They work with residents, businesses, and other organizations to deliver agreed-upon services. To fund these services, they generate revenue from various sources. These include funding from the national government, taxes, fees, and charges collected from local people and businesses.

Local museums are often either run by local authorities or receive local government support.

Public restrooms are managed and maintained by local authorities.

Bus stops ensure that people have access to local shops and services.

Burials are arranged by local authorities for people who have no next of kin.

Marriage licensing office ensure that any wedding between two people is lega recognized by the state.

Schools and colleges are often funded and maintained by local governments.

Community safety initiatives, such as crime prevention strategies, are managed by local groups.

Allotments, or community gardens, may be made available by groups for people to rent.

LOCAL AND NATIONAL GOVERNMENT

Governing a country involves balancing the powers of national and local governments. In decentralized systems, local governments are considered best placed to meet the needs of their communities. They are usually allocated greater resources and given more autonomy to make decisions and prioritize different policies. In centralized systems, however, local governments have less autonomy and largely carry out decisions made by the national government.

Parks and recreational facilities are maintained by local authorities for people's leisure, entertainment, and recreational pursuits.

Social care is delivered or commissioned by local groups for people who need extra support.

Sports centers and swimming pools are often either run or supported by local authorities to enhance people's health and well-being.

The town hall is the principal administrative building of the local authority.

Public libraries are usually run by local governments and provide access to books, music, and other services.

Licenses are provided to businesses to permit them to conduct specific business activities in the community.

Markets and fairs can be opened by groups to stimulate the local economy.

Solar panels and other green energy devices may be subsidized by local governments.

Business rates are charged by local governments on most non-residential properties, including shops and offices.

Recycling services are usually organized by the local government to help reduce waste and protect the environment.

Houses may be rented by local authorities, which may also provide housing support for citizens.

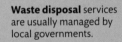

Waste disposal services are usually managed by local governments.

Roads and road maintenance are essential for ensuring that people can travel safely.

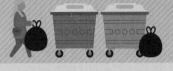

Planning regulations ensure that construction work is done in accordance with local policies.

Nongovernmental organizations

NGOs are nonprofit agencies set up by citizens, and they operate independently of government and politics to serve the public interest and advance social well-being.

Humanitarian interests

There is no single definition of "nongovernmental organizations" (NGOs); however, there is a range of characteristics associated with them. The term typically refers to organizations set up by citizens working for humanitarian rather than commercial interests (NGOs usually do not seek to make a profit). They are independent of government and other state influences, although they may receive government funding or collaborate with governmental departments. They can operate for the benefit of members (a grassroots organization) or for the benefit of others (an agency). Areas in which NGOs typically operate include human rights, poverty, development, climate change, and the environment in addition to health, disability, and education. NGOs can focus on these issues at a local, national, or global level.

Some countries use the word "charity" to describe nongovernmental organizations, although not all NGOs have legal charitable status.

What NGOs do

There are two broad categories of NGO: operational and advocacy. Operational NGOs design and implement specific interventions, often filling the gap where certain public services are not provided by local authorities. This can include delivering education, health, and training services as well as providing infrastructure, such as schools, wells, and public toilets, and building housing.

10m

NGOs are thought to be currently operating worldwide.

https://worldngoday.org, "What is an NGO?" (2021)

Advocacy NGOs seek to promote a specific cause. They do this by raising awareness about an issue in order to bring about change. They may seek to alter government policy or law (on human rights, for example) or to change people's attitudes on a given issue, such as female genital mutilation. They use various approaches to do this, from campaigning and lobbying, to soliciting the media, to engaging in activism. Some NGOs may have operational and advocacy functions.

A BRIEF HISTORY OF NGOS

The term "nongovernmental organization" was first popularized in the 1945 founding charter of the United Nations. However, NGOs existed long before then, with roots in the religious organizations and social movements that emerged in the US and Europe after the Industrial Revolution. The Anti-Slavery Society, formed in 1839, is considered the first international NGO. The end of the Cold War in the late 1980s and the wave of democratization that followed led to a boom in NGOs.

The diversity of NGOs

There is great variation in the types of NGO. Some are small, with no income and a few volunteers working on an issue affecting a local community. Others have budgets of millions of dollars, with hundreds of highly trained staff working in offices around the world on global issues. NGOs also vary according to funding sources and how closely they work with the governments of the countries in which they operate.

SIZE OF NGO

Many NGOs are small-scale volunteer-run organizations that work within a specific community, either campaigning on local issues or providing basic but essential services.

Larger NGOs, with a mix of professional and voluntary staff, typically operate across a country, either providing essential services or working on nationwide campaigns.

The best-known NGOs operate internationally, typically working on global issues. One high-profile example is the human rights organization Amnesty International.

TYPES OF ISSUES

Local issues
The issues that local NGOs focus on might include preventing a library closure, protecting green spaces, or providing language support to refugees.

National issues
National NGOs might be involved in lobbying to change government policy on specific issues, such as adult literacy or sexual health.

International issues
Global NGOs often address global concerns, such as climate change, or specialize in emergency responses to war, famine, or natural disasters.

SOURCES OF FUNDING

Own funding
Many NGOs, large and small, source their own funding through private donations, sales of goods and services, or membership dues.

Government funding
NGO funding from government sources can take various forms, such as grants, foreign aid for work in low-income countries, or payment for specific services.

International funding
Global NGOs may receive funding from international bodies, such as the EU or the UN, or from large philanthropic organizations.

PROXIMITY TO GOVERNMENT

Independent of government
Smaller operational NGOs may have little interaction with high-level officialdom because they are often working in areas with little government presence.

Government cooperation
NGOs can work with national governments in various ways, providing expert advice, delivering key services, or collaborating to deliver change.

In opposition to government
Some NGOs apply pressure in order to highlight injustices. This can mean reporting on or publicly protesting against certain government policies.

POLITICAL CHANGE

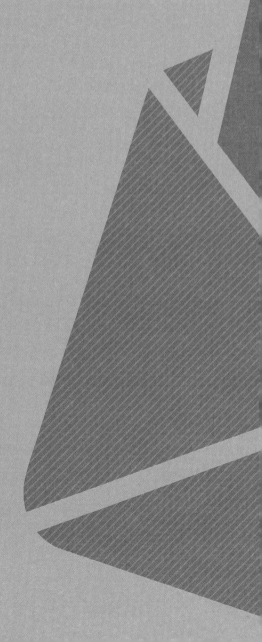

Elections and voting

Elections exist to enable citizens to choose whom they want to be governed by. This means voting for individuals or a political party who will represent the citizens' interests in their legislature. Elections are not confined to parliaments and also occur in town councils, trade unions, community groups, business corporations, and other organizations. Countries ruled by authoritarian regimes may sometimes hold elections, but typically these are not fair and free and are held only for show.

Why we have elections

Kofi Annan (1938–2018), the former Secretary-General of the United Nations, said that elections are the "indispensable root of democracy." To put it another way, they are the tool that enables democracy to function. Not only do voters get to select their leaders, but citizens can also hold those leaders to account by voting them out of office at the end of their term if they have performed badly. In most cases, elections also enable a peaceful transfer of power.

Credibility

To be credible, elections must be inclusive, transparent, and fair. However, many elections fall short of these criteria (see pp.114–15).

"When the electorate believes elections have been free and fair, they can be a powerful catalyst for better governance."

Kofi Annan, foreword to *Deepening Democracy* (2012)

ALTERNATIVES TO ELECTIONS

Critics of the election process point out that after having cast their vote, citizens have no further involvement in the democratic process until they are called to vote again some years later. Meanwhile, politicians make decisions without reference to the electorate. This can result in public distrust of elected politicians and governments and an unwillingness to engage in the electoral process, which results in low voter turnout. Alternatives to elections might include people's assemblies, in which interested citizens debate important issues, and sortition—the random selection of political officials from a large pool of candidates.

Voting

Only eligible citizens can vote; there are usually age or other restrictions. Voting is voluntary in most countries, although it is compulsory in a few.

Fixed term

The period between elections varies, but elected governments are required to return to the voters at fixed intervals to extend their stay in office or to be replaced.

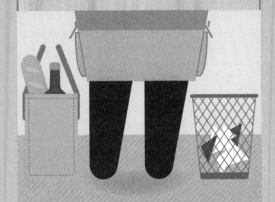

Election campaigns

Campaigns are the means by which political parties and their candidates present their ideas and positions on key issues to voters in the run-up to polling day.

Informing the voters

The political campaign is at the heart of the democratic electoral process. It is the time when the public has the opportunity to learn about the character, beliefs, and values of those who aspire to govern them. At the same time, campaigns provide candidates and political parties with the chance to promote themselves and their ideologies to the electorate.

The candidates use a variety of methods, traditionally including printed material, interviews, and public appearances, and, in more recent times, social media. They may use polling to identify "swing" (undecided) voters so that they can allocate resources to winning them over. The dates of an official election campaign period are often legally defined and can be anything from a month to much longer: in the US presidential election of 2016, Ted Cruz, first to enter the race, announced his candidacy 596 days before election day.

Campaigning is strictly regulated, particularly with regard to spending, in order to maintain fairness. The intention is that citizens should be sufficiently well informed that they are able to choose the candidate who best represents their interests.

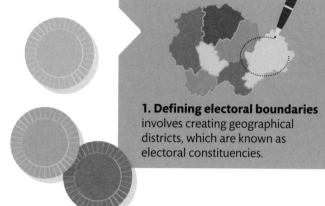

1. Defining electoral boundaries involves creating geographical districts, which are known as electoral constituencies.

7. Blackout periods in some countries end campaigning hours before polling begins.

Election timetable

The electoral process begins long before the candidates start their campaigns. Matters such as who can vote and where must be decided, as well as the lineup of candidates. Once the campaigns end and voting takes place, the announcement of the results should follow quickly. However, there is always the risk of a contested result, as occurred in the US presidential election of 2000, Bush vs. Gore, which required a month-long process to determine the winner.

8. Polling day is when citizens cast their votes at a designated polling station, although some may vote early by mail or online.

9. Counting of votes takes place when all polling stations have closed. It may be done by hand or, more recently, electronically.

2. Political party nominations take place early to identify the candidates who will run in the election.

3. Voter registration establishes who is eligible to vote and stores their details on an electoral roll. Anyone who is not on the roll cannot vote.

4. Campaign finances are subject to rules governing how much can be spent; this ensures that all parties have an equal chance.

6. Campaigning gives candidates the opportunity to communicate directly with the electorate in various ways, from social media to personal appearances at rallies.

5. Manifestos or political platforms outline party policies and commitments.

10. The results come in at different times and are usually announced as they arrive, until an overall winner can be determined.

11. Disputed results can prevent the formation of a government, or at least undermine its legitimacy if the issue is not resolved.

"A national political campaign is better than the best circus ever heard of."

H. L. Mencken, American journalist,
A Prairie Home Companion (2015)

Electoral systems

An electoral system is the process that determines how people vote in an election and how the results are interpreted. There are several types of electoral systems, each of which has pros and cons.

Election rules

The right to vote to elect someone into public office is considered fundamental to democracy. The practice has existed since the 6th century BCE, when it was introduced into the Greek city-state of Athens.

The set of rules that governs how elections are run, voted on, and concluded is referred to as an electoral system. Today, there are a number of electoral systems, which rule on the method of voting that is used during a political election and are incorporated into a constitution of electoral law.

Electoral systems dictate every aspect of the voting process, from who is eligible to vote or stand as a candidate to where polling booths are located, the use of proxy votes (when someone votes on behalf of someone else) or postal votes, and the timing of the election. They also determine how voting slips are marked, how they are counted, and the way in which the votes will establish the final outcome.

Different systems

The types of electoral systems used vary from country to country. They include plurality systems, which

Types of voting

Two of the most common forms of voting are proportional representation (PR), in which the election of political candidates is based on the proportion of the vote they receive, and first-past-the-post (FPTP), where successful candidates achieve a simple majority. Some countries, such as Germany and New Zealand, use the Additional Member System, which combines PR with the election of local candidates.

"Nothing is more unreliable than the populace... nothing more deceptive than the whole electoral system."

Marcus Tullius Cicero, Roman statesman

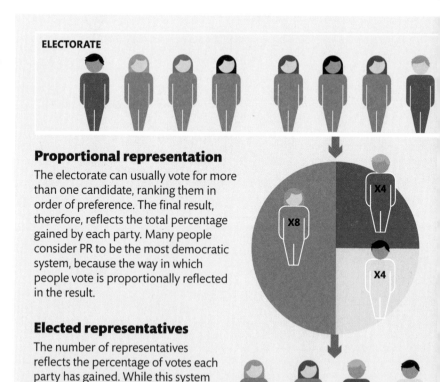

ELECTORATE

Proportional representation

The electorate can usually vote for more than one candidate, ranking them in order of preference. The final result, therefore, reflects the total percentage gained by each party. Many people consider PR to be the most democratic system, because the way in which people vote is proportionally reflected in the result.

Elected representatives

The number of representatives reflects the percentage of votes each party has gained. While this system enables minority parties to be represented, critics argue that no party ever receives an overall majority.

elect candidates with the most votes (but not necessarily with a majority); majoritarian systems, which require a majority of votes to win; and proportional systems, which aim for elected representatives to reflect wider public support.

Variations exist within these categories. The voting method first-past-the-post (FPTP) is a widely used system that tends to favor the major political parties. Another method is proportional representation (PR), which supporters argue reflects voters' preferences more accurately.

SYSTEMS AROUND THE WORLD

More than a third of the world's countries use either a majority or a plurality system, including the US and the UK. The use of proportional representation is favored by the vast majority of European countries.

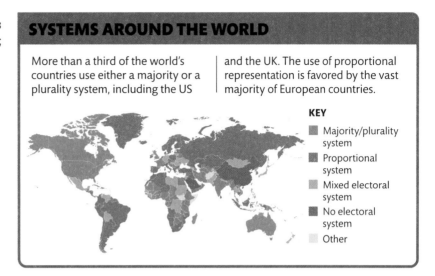

KEY
- Majority/plurality system
- Proportional system
- Mixed electoral system
- No electoral system
- Other

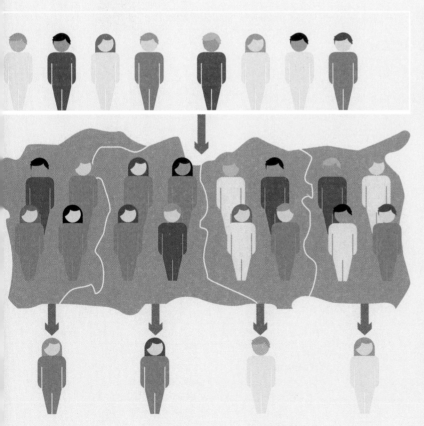

Electorate
The body of people in a country who are eligible to vote is known as the electorate. Unless voting is mandatory, it is rare for 100 percent of the electorate to vote.

First-past-the-post
The electorate can only vote for one candidate on their ballot sheet, even though many may be listed from other parties. The final result is based on one candidate, or party, achieving a majority, irrespective of turnout. This may mean a candidate wins on less than a 50 percent turnout, while smaller parties are ignored.

Elected representatives
With FPTP, one party can gain more electoral seats despite having fewer overall votes. It favors large political parties; minority parties, even if they poll well, are unlikely to gain seats. Many feel FPTP invalidates their vote.

Referendums

An example of direct democracy in action, referendums invite citizens to say yes or no to a particular political issue rather than leaving the decision making to elected representatives.

Voting on specifics

The most important aspect of a referendum is that the electorate (those citizens eligible to vote) are asked to decide on a specific issue. This distinguishes a referendum from an election (see pp.106–07), where the electorate cast their votes for a parliamentary candidate who will represent them and vote on their behalf. A referendum is therefore a public vote, usually one that requires a simple yes or no answer.

Referendums can be employed for a variety of reasons. In some countries, including Austria and many Latin American nations, it is a legal obligation to hold a referendum on any proposed amendments to the constitution. Referendums have frequently been used as a tool for independence or self-determination movements. In 1993, Eritrea, then part of Ethiopia, held a referendum on independence. Turnout was more than 98 percent, of which 99.8 percent voted in favor of going it alone; Eritrea declared independence two days later. In 2017, the region of Catalonia held a referendum on independence from Spain, and 92 percent voted in

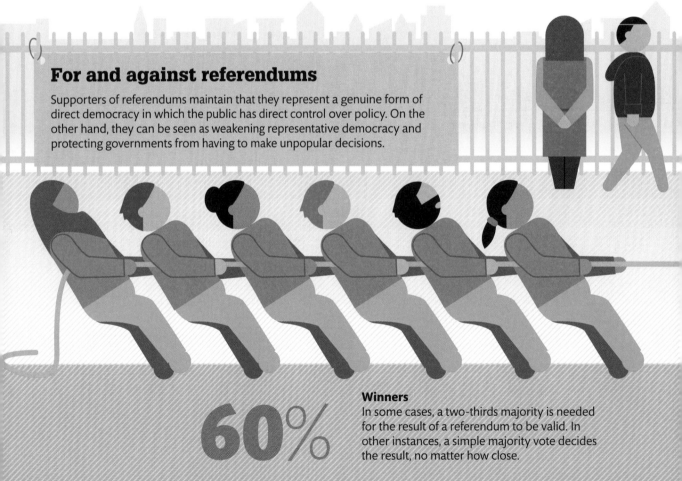

For and against referendums

Supporters of referendums maintain that they represent a genuine form of direct democracy in which the public has direct control over policy. On the other hand, they can be seen as weakening representative democracy and protecting governments from having to make unpopular decisions.

60%

Winners
In some cases, a two-thirds majority is needed for the result of a referendum to be valid. In other instances, a simple majority vote decides the result, no matter how close.

favor; however, the Spanish government declared the referendum unconstitutional.

Many countries rarely hold referendums; others hold them frequently. Switzerland makes more use of referendums than any other country in the world.

Referendums can get people interested in politics in a way that representative democracy generally does not. But they can be used by politicians keen to avoid making difficult and unpopular decisions. Wins by only a narrow margin can also foster division within a nation.

600
referendums have been held in Switzerland since it became a modern state in 1848.

www.swissinfo.ch, "How direct democracy has grown over the decades" (2018)

CASE STUDY

Brexit

The UK rarely holds referendums, but in 2016, the government held one on the question of whether the country should remain a member of the EU or leave the EU. It was contentious, not least because it offered a binary choice: remain or leave. Turnout was high, and the result was close: 51.89 percent voted leave, 48.11 percent remain. In 2020, Britain left the EU, but the country remains politically divided.

Turnout
In some instances, as occurred in the 2006 independence referendum in Montenegro, a specified percentage of electors may be needed to validate the result.

Government
The government determines when a referendum takes place and which form it takes: a simple yes-no vote or multiple choices.

YES   NO

The outcome
The result is seen as a statement of public opinion that can be used to settle what may be a controversial issue. The government can act on the outcome.

Losers
If the outcome is close on a controversial issue, the matter may not be considered ended, allowing for the possibility of further referendums.

40%

Manipulating elections

Democratic elections should be transparent and fair, but this is not always the case. Elections are sometimes manipulated to ensure the success of a particular candidate or political party.

Misleading the electorate

There are numerous ways to subvert the election process. Some are relatively subtle, such as redrawing constituency boundaries to influence the outcome of a vote (a practice that has been employed even in some countries considered to have strong and fair democratic traditions). Other methods are cruder—for instance, the arrest of opposition politicians and threats of violence against their supporters, which can occur in elections held in more authoritarian countries.

Shaping the flow of information on the Internet has become a key strategy in influencing the outcome of elections (see pp.122–23). Online discussions can be manipulated in favor of a particular party; access to news sources, communication tools, and, in some cases, the entire Internet can be restricted; and alternative facts can be presented in what is known as "fake news."

Preventing such fraud is proving to be difficult. Possible safeguards include tightening electoral law and monitoring by independent bodies, such as nongovernmental organizations. Some countries use voter identity cards with built-in security mechanisms, but there is a danger that such measures can deprive some people of their right to vote if they do not carry the "correct" identification.

Disenfranchisement

Applying conditions of residency, literacy, or ethnicity means groups such as the homeless cannot vote.

Gerrymandering

This involves redrawing electoral boundaries to the advantage of one party. It may also involve relocating ethnic groups.

Obstacles to voting

Casting a vote should be simple, but there are sometimes barriers, many of which affect disadvantaged members of society, who are least likely to vote to maintain the status quo. Examples include a requirement to have identification that uses officially sanctioned photos, not available to everyone, or a ruling that prevents people from a particular ethnic background or those who are illiterate from voting.

Vote buying

This is when people are offered something in exchange for their vote. In Venezuela in 2018, the poor were offered food for votes.

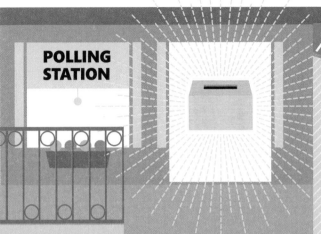

POLLING STATION

CASE STUDY

Cambridge Analytica

In 2018, it emerged that a British consulting firm, Cambridge Analytica, had been collecting online personal data without consent. The data were obtained through an app, which consisted of questions designed to create psychological profiles. The information was used to build up voter profiles that could be sold to political campaigns. The profiles were used to assist the 2016 presidential campaigns of Ted Cruz and Donald Trump in the US. Data provided by Cambridge Analytica is thought to have played a role in influencing around around 200 elections worldwide.

Disinformation

Spreading fake news in order to discredit opponents and manipulating polling data are now common electoral tools.

Ballot fraud

This includes falsifying, destroying, or deliberately losing ballots (the paper slips marked with the voter's preference).

Intimidation

Of all the elections that took place globally in 2020, more than half were marred by some form of violence.

Ballot stuffing

People casting multiple votes is known as ballot stuffing. This was reportedly done by supporters of Vladimir Putin in Russia in 2021.

Destruction of ballots

Destroying ballot papers is difficult to do without being noticed, but these can be secretly defaced so they become invalid.

Refusal to accept results

In 2011, Nigerian candidate Muhammadu Buhari refused to concede defeat, as did Donald Trump in the US in 2020.

The media in politics

The media plays a key role in politics. Its job is to keep the public informed about current affairs and to provide platforms for politicians, who can both express themselves and be scrutinized. In the past, the media was made up of newspapers and a handful of radio and television channels, but there is now also a huge online presence, along with digital services. Increasingly, traditional media also faces competition from amateur citizen journalists.

Newspapers

Although newspapers continue to lose readers to other forms of media, they remain influential in politics, as individual journals lend their weight to a particular political party or ideology.

Television

Television remains a powerful tool for shaping political opinion. Some channels pride themselves on their objectivity, while others may be state-owned or have a definite political agenda.

STIRRING UP THE PEOPLE

The viral nature of social media makes it an effective tool for political dissent. For instance, social media platforms played a key role in the popular uprisings known as the Arab Spring, which swept North Africa and the Middle East in 2010 to 2012. Similarly, social media was used as a tool in the 2019–2020 Hong Kong protests against the Chinese government. Social media allowed demonstrators to spread information and organize protest actions while concealing their identities and avoiding detainment by the police. They also used social media as a tool in the battle for public opinion—for instance, by circulating images and footage of police brutality.

> "We are the United States of Amnesia... [the] media... has no desire to tell us the truth."
>
> Gore Vidal, American writer, *Imperial America* (2004)

Bloggers

The Internet allows individuals a platform to not only express political opinion but also bring key information to public attention and shape popular discourse.

Websites

In addition to online versions of print newspapers, there is an increasing number of dedicated, online-only political sites, some of which—*HuffPost*, for example—wield considerable influence.

Social media

Political news sites and bloggers can break and shape stories, but nothing spreads those stories—and therefore influences public opinion—faster than the various social media platforms.

Setting the agenda

Traditionally, the media has had two key roles: setting the news agenda by choosing which stories to present to the public; and shaping public opinion through the way it presents and comments on those stories. Today, however, millions of people have cameras on their phones and mobile access to the Internet, both of which enable them to report on events that the mainstream media may have ignored. The ability of citizen journalists to bring to the world's attention otherwise unreported events has raised questions regarding the future relevance of traditional media.

Freedom of the press

In order to make informed decisions at elections, people need to have free access to information about their governments, which in turn requires that the press is free from government control.

A universal right

According to the United Nations' Universal Declaration of Human Rights (see pp.124–25), every human being has the right to freedom of opinion and expression. This includes the freedom to seek and receive information through any media, regardless of borders.

Produced just after World War II, this declaration restated the classical liberal idea that in order for people to make educated decisions at elections, they must have free access to information. This freedom guarantees that the information circulating in a society is not simply propaganda produced by the government but is a mixture of opinions, including critiques of the government made by professional journalists and ordinary citizens. However, having press freedom does not mean that the public is able to learn every detail about a government's decisions. Legally, the government may classify certain documents as "secret" for the sake of the nation's interest, although it may later release them for public scrutiny. Freedom of information legislation, which many countries have, determines what kind of information can be withheld from the public in this way, and under what circumstances. According to the nonprofit organization Reporters Without Borders, around a third of the world's population lives in countries where governments heavily influence what the press reports. In the organization's 2021 report, it was revealed that the countries with the least press freedom were Eritrea, North Korea, Turkmenistan, and China. By contrast, countries where the press had the most freedom were Norway, Finland, Sweden, and Denmark.

Getting to the truth

Having a free press guarantees that the citizens of a country are not simply bombarded by state propaganda. However, this does not mean that newspapers, television news channels, and other media outlets are impartial. Each outlet may have its own agenda and even advertise which political viewpoint it represents. This enables citizens to engage in debate and to decide for themselves which viewpoint best represents their own interests or the interests of society.

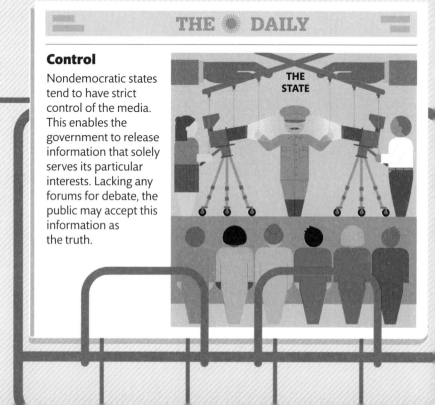

THE ☀ DAILY

Control

Nondemocratic states tend to have strict control of the media. This enables the government to release information that solely serves its particular interests. Lacking any forums for debate, the public may accept this information as the truth.

THE STATE

THE ☀ DAILY

Freedom

In truly democratic countries, the media is free from state control. This enables the public to scrutinize public officials and to decide for themselves which politicians best represent their interests and whom they should vote for in elections.

"If liberty means anything at all, it means the right to tell people what they do not want to hear."

George Orwell, British writer, from an unpublished preface to *Animal Farm* (1945)

THE ☀ DAILY

Analysis

Press freedom enables citizens to analyze the biases of media outlets. The press can also publish information about public officials that may include details of how politicians are funded during elections.

 CASE STUDY

Charlie Hebdo

On January 7, 2015, two French men entered the offices of the satirical magazine *Charlie Hebdo* in Paris and shot at its employees, killing 12 people and injuring 11 others. The gunmen's stated motive was to avenge the magazine's publication of cartoons of the Prophet Muhammad—an act that was considered highly offensive by many Muslims. The killings highlighted the question of whether freedom of expression—and, therefore, the freedom of the press—is an absolute right or whether it should be tempered by concern for the sensitivities of religious groups.

Propaganda and censorship

Even the most democratic governments try to influence public opinion, whether by exposing the lies behind false information, censoring unwanted views, or deliberately withholding facts from the public.

Persuading the public

Governments have always been interested in controlling information. Doing so enables them to justify decisions that might otherwise be unpopular with the public, such as raising taxes or going to war, and to reduce the amount of false claims that an opposition group might make about their policies. They may also do so to ensure that sensitive information concerning national security remains secret.

Historically, governments have had two main means of controlling information. The first of these is propaganda, which is a biased form of communication that seeks to promote a particular point of view by appealing to people's emotions rather than their rationality. The second method is censorship—suppressing information that the state considers dangerous for the public to know (see pp.118–19).

In recent decades, technology has made it much more difficult for governments to use these tools. In particular, the Internet has enabled people to fact-check government statements and to

Controlling public opinion

When faced with crises, governments often do whatever they can to explain what is happening, both to their own populations and to the world at large. Even when a government is not to blame for a crisis, it will tend to stress its successes in responding to events and downplay its failures and so could be criticized for not being wholly truthful with the public. However, governments may also lie about events, which can lead them to suppress news outlets that may contradict their official story. For similar reasons, authoritarian regimes may permanently control their populations' access to information.

Propaganda
All governments try to emphasize how effective they are. For example, during health crises, they tend to publicize only their successes in responding to protect the public.

Scapegoating
When an authoritarian regime causes a crisis, it may blame foreign governments for the situation and may arrest any of its citizens who question its version of events.

source a variety of alternative points of view. For this reason, the Internet is either banned or severely restricted in countries that are dominated by a single political party, such as China, North Korea, and Iran (see pp.74–75). In these countries, posters and films of party leaders still play a dominant role in political life, encouraging personality cults that might be undermined if the public had full access to the Internet.

Controlling the Internet

Although censorship is a key feature of one-party states, it still plays a vital role in democratic countries. Because, in principle,

anyone can post anything they want on the Internet, governments have an interest in ensuring that fake news is kept to a minimum. In particular, they invest a lot of money in technologies that can filter Internet service providers that are known to be used by criminal organizations or political extremists (see pp.182–83).

Most governments monitor social media platforms, fining operators who contravene national laws. Some may also attempt to suppress views considered to be too controversial. In this sense, few countries in the world can be said to offer totally unregulated access to the Internet.

CASE STUDY

North Korea

In North Korea, the only news outlets that are available to the public are state-run news agencies, and these spend a large portion of their resources promoting the Kim dynasty, which has ruled the country since 1948. Between 2004 and 2008, cellular devices were completely banned, and since then, only a small elite has had 3G cellular access. High-ranking officials have limited access to the Internet, and use of the country's intranet is carefully monitored.

NEWS

BREAKING NEWS:

ERODING LIBERTY...

Censorship

Most governments censor the Internet to some extent, though they may not disclose what is blocked. China has a highly sophisticated censorship system that can filter search terms and block dissent.

NO SIGNAL

Shutdown

Authoritarian regimes often shut down the Internet to silence protest groups. Iran, Cuba, Chad, Kazakhstan, Jordan, and Myanmar are among the many countries that have done so recently.

67%

of Internet users live in countries in which criticism of the government is censored.

Freedom House report (2016)

Social media and misinformation

Because it is largely unregulated, social media can be a minefield of misinformation and fake news. At its worst, it can create isolated communities that rely on biased newsfeeds for information.

Misinformation

According to a 2021 survey from think tank the Pew Research Center, more than half (53 percent) of US adults claimed to access news stories through social media. The same survey shows that using social media as a source of news is most popular with younger age groups, suggesting that this trend will increase. At the same time, social media has proven to be a major conduit for misinformation—both unintentional and intentional.

Unintentional misinformation arises when news stories on social media originate from a single source, with no form of fact-checking or corroboration. There are also individuals, agencies, and organizations who are thought to intentionally distribute inaccurate information in a bid to sway opinions and outcomes. Examples such as the Cambridge Analytica scandal (see pp.114–15) show that people's online profiles and behaviors can be tracked in order to develop effective psychological targeting that can influence their attitudes and decision making.

Polarization

Research has shown that articles containing misinformation are also among the most viral. In other words, fake news spreads faster than the truth: the more outrageous the content, the more people are thought to share it.

Social media users tend to engage with other users who have similar views: conservatives tend to interact with other conservatives, and liberals with other liberals. This is reinforced by social media platforms' algorithms, which link users of similar beliefs, creating "filter bubbles." In this way, social media can polarize the electorate and undermine debate.

Social media platforms have been slow to confront misinformation. One reason is that there is so much content that it has become almost impossible to police it all. Critics also highlight that these platforms depend on continued use and that misinformation gets "clicks."

TYPES OF MISINFORMATION

There are numerous forms of misinformation, most of which are designed to deceive the reader into believing something that may not be true.

> **False connection** is when headlines or imagery do not support the content of the piece.

> **False context** is when genuine content is shared with false contextual information.

> **Manipulated content** is when genuine information or imagery is manipulated in order to deceive.

> **Satire or parody** is when information is meant as a joke but still has the potential to fool those who do not recognize it as such.

> **Misleading content** is when information is used in a misleading way to frame an issue or individual.

> **Imposter content** is when genuine sources are impersonated, so that, for example, a web page pretends to be the official representation of an agency or individual, when in fact it is not.

> **Fabricated content** is new content that is entirely false and purposefully designed to deceive and do harm.

Filter bubbles

Algorithms devised by social media platforms dictate the newsfeeds and search results presented to online users. By determining which content a user is more likely to engage with, the platform filters out any news that might present an opposing point of view or issues in which a user has not shown any previous interest. As a result, the information to which the user is exposed is significantly biased.

News stories

Once a news story is published online, it is picked up and filtered according to various algorithms employed by search engines and social media feeds.

Feedback

The algorithm learns and adapts to an individual user's online behavior and makes any necessary adjustments.

Algorithms

These are mathematical sets of rules that assess data based on a user's personal preferences and previous engagement online.

Rejected stories

If a story does not fit a user's profile—as determined by the algorithm—it is rejected and not displayed on any of that person's online feeds.

Accepted story

If an algorithm decides that a news story fits a user's profile, it will push it into the user's feed.

User

If the user "likes" or shares a story, this will mean that they receive more of the same in the future.

FEEDBACK

Matching content

Algorithms will offer similar news stories and note which the user engages with and how.

Shared stories

Every story a user shares with friends shapes the "filter bubble" of that particular community.

Friends

Algorithms are also sensitive to stories shared by a user's friends.

Rights

Rights are understood to be those things that people are morally or legally entitled to have or to do. Among these are the right to life, the right to vote, and the right to work. Some question whether rights really exist, given that they are not universally applied and are often violated. Yet the idea of rights is fundamental to the way people live—shaping our laws, our governments, and our perceptions of morality while also helping protect freedoms.

The evolution of rights

The idea that people are entitled to basic rights that are not dependent on the law, customs, or government emerged during the Enlightenment (see p.17), which inspired revolutions in both the US and France. Over time, this notion of universal rights has spread around the world, transforming the relationship between governments and individuals.

The ancient Greeks

Philosophers in ancient Greece had rudimentary ideas about rights—particularly those linked to the idea that all humans are subject to a basic law of nature.

Enlightenment thinkers

Thinkers such as Thomas Hobbes and John Locke (see pp.12–13) conceived of natural rights that are not dependent on the laws or customs of a particular culture but are considered universal and inalienable.

The US Constitution

The US Constitution (1787) was influential on the matter of human rights. The first 10 amendments spell out Americans' rights in relation to their government.

"Peace **can** only last **where** human rights are respected... **and where** individuals **and** nations are free."

Tenzin Gyatso, 14th Dalai Lama, Nobel Peace Prize acceptance speech (1989)

UNIVERSAL DECLARATION OF HUMAN RIGHTS

Following World War II and the horrors of the Holocaust, world governments met in 1948 to adopt the Universal Declaration of Human Rights (UDHR), which enshrined the rights of all human beings. The declaration consists of 30 articles detailing individuals' basic rights and freedoms, regardless of "nationality, place of residence, gender, national or ethnic origin, color, religion, language, or any other status." Although not legally binding, the declaration's contents have been incorporated into subsequent international treaties, national constitutions, and legal codes.

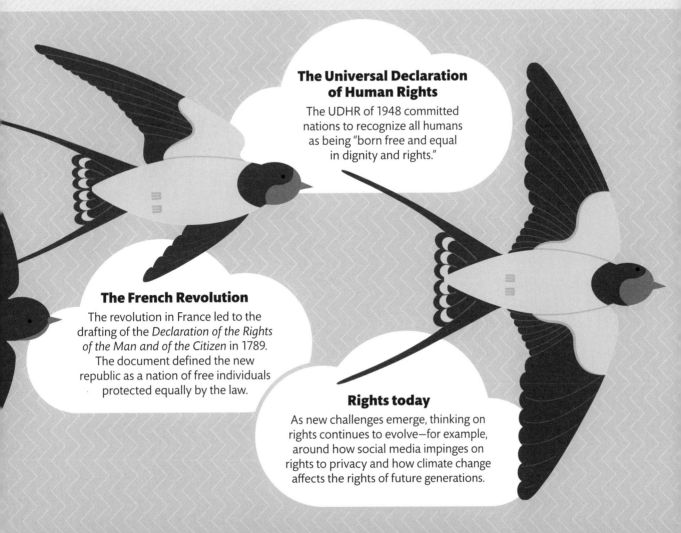

The Universal Declaration of Human Rights

The UDHR of 1948 committed nations to recognize all humans as being "born free and equal in dignity and rights."

The French Revolution

The revolution in France led to the drafting of the *Declaration of the Rights of the Man and of the Citizen* in 1789. The document defined the new republic as a nation of free individuals protected equally by the law.

Rights today

As new challenges emerge, thinking on rights continues to evolve—for example, around how social media impinges on rights to privacy and how climate change affects the rights of future generations.

Human, moral, and legal rights

Rights can be categorized in different ways: there are significant distinctions to be made between human, moral, and legal rights, which differ according to their aims and their impact.

Types of rights

Human rights are thought of as universal rights inherent to all human beings, irrespective of race, nationality, sex, religion, or any other distinguishing characteristic. These rights are inalienable, meaning they cannot be taken away from people by governments.

Legal rights are rights that are granted by the state to its citizens. They are recognized and protected by the law. Legal rights can be repealed or removed by governments. They are not universal; instead, they vary across countries and can change over time. There are penalties for violations of legal rights.

Moral rights are awarded to people according to an ethical or moral code. They are based on notions of what is right and correct. Like human rights, moral rights are considered universal and timeless. They are thought to be morally correct for the common good of humanity and so are not determined by the state. However, there is no penalty for moral rights violations.

Why is it necessary to consider these different types of rights? Some people argue that only legal rights matter, as these are enshrined in law and there is some punishment for violating them. Others disagree, arguing that moral rights are just as important. For example, under South Africa's system of apartheid, among many other forms of discrimination, Black South Africans were not allowed to vote, and so they had no legal right to full political participation.

LEGAL RIGHT
In most countries, there is no legal right to be rescued. If a person fails to rescue another person, they will not be prosecuted.

Legal or moral?

There are many instances where legal and moral rights overlap. For example, a person's right to life is considered both a moral and a legal right, just as murder is both morally wrong and illegal. However, there are instances when moral and legal rights differ. If someone falls into a lake and is drowning, most people would expect a passerby to try to rescue that individual; however, the right to be saved is not always an enforceable right.

However, there was international recognition of Black South Africans' moral right to political participation, and the apartheid laws were viewed as morally wrong. Opposition to apartheid arose because it violated the moral rights of Black South African people rather than their legal rights.

This example demonstrates why human rights cannot be exclusively reduced to legal rights—it would prevent people from condemning unjust systems from a rights perspective. Instead, human rights can be considered to be both moral and legal rights. The legitimacy of human rights comes because they are moral rights, but their practical use depends on their being developed into legal rights.

✓ NEED TO KNOW

> **Universality** means something that is true for all individuals, regardless of culture, sex, race, religion, or any other distinguishing feature.

> **Morality** refers to a system of values and principles of conduct. These principles establish the extent to which an action is right or wrong and distinguish between good and bad behavior.

> **Legality** refers to whether an action, agreement, or contract is consistent with the law—in other words, whether it is legal or illegal.

MORAL RIGHT
Most people would agree, however, that there is a moral right to be rescued—a passerby should try to save a drowning person.

MORAL TO LEGAL
Some countries have introduced "duty to rescue" laws stating that people must give reasonable assistance to those in peril.

Negative and positive rights

Some rights impose an obligation on others. Negative rights oblige others (or the state) to refrain from certain actions, while positive rights oblige others (or the state) to perform certain actions.

Action and inaction

An example of a negative right that a government might infringe on is the right of an individual not to be imprisoned without a fair trial. Likewise, an individual's positive right might be violated if a government failed to provide them with health care, social services, or education. In these cases, the person's rights are violated by government action and inaction, respectively.

The differences between such action and inaction have been used to categorize different kinds of rights. A negative right is a person's right not to be subjected to certain actions by others or the state. A positive right is a person's right to be provided with something through the action of others or the state. Negative rights are typically those that are linked to people's political and civil rights, such as freedom of speech; positive rights are generally economic or social rights, such as the right to health care. The constitutions of liberal democracies usually provide protection for negative rights, but not necessarily for positive rights—although these are often protected by specific laws, particularly in countries that have welfare states.

Critics argue that the distinction between negative and positive rights is often artificial and arbitrary. For example, the right to own private property is typically defined as a negative right (people have the right not to be prevented from owning property), but this negative right must be actively protected by the state.

Rights and obligations

A "right" refers to a person's entitlement to have or do something, while the "obligation" is what must be done for that right to be realized. Sometimes the obligation to fulfill one person's rights may interfere with the rights of another.

Negative rights and obligations

A person's negative right is the right not to be subjected to certain actions by the government. Therefore, a person's negative rights oblige the state not to interfere in that person's life.

NEGATIVE RIGHTS
If a person chooses to grow oranges on their property, their negative rights mean that they have the right to produce and sell oranges to whomever they choose, without interference.

OBLIGATIONS
The obligation on the part of the government would be to leave that person to produce oranges and let them do whatever they choose with the fruit.

> "A right is not effectual by itself, but only in relation to the obligation to which it corresponds."

Simone Weil, French philosopher, *L'Enracinement* (1949)

BERLIN'S TWO CONCEPTS OF LIBERTY

The concept of positive and negative rights is often confused with those of positive and negative liberty proposed by British philosopher Isaiah Berlin (1909–1997). Negative liberty is similar to the concept of negative rights in that both refer to freedom from external interference. However, positive rights and positive liberty are very different: a positive right is the right to something, while positive liberty refers to a person's freedom to act on their free will.

Positive rights and obligations

A person's positive right is the right to be provided with particular goods or services. It places an obligation on the government to act to provide its citizens with these goods or services.

Conflicts

By protecting one person's positive rights, the state could infringe on the negative rights of someone else. Similarly, by respecting the negative rights of a person, the state may violate the negative rights of another. Hence, conflicts between sets of rights can arise.

POSITIVE RIGHTS
A person's positive rights would include the right not to go hungry, which means that they should receive—or have access to—food.

OBLIGATIONS
The obligation on the part of the government to meet this right would be to provide the person with necessary food or access to it.

COMPETING RIGHTS
For the government to safeguard the positive rights of a hungry person, it may take oranges that another person has grown, violating their negative rights.

The citizens' right to vote

A defining feature of democracies is that all adult citizens have the right to vote for their political representatives. However, in most countries, this right was only won after long struggles to overcome voting restrictions.

Universal suffrage

The right of all adult citizens to vote in elections, or "universal suffrage," is a fundamental feature of democratic systems. Free and fair elections with good voter participation ensure genuine competition for power in society.

In most countries today, all adults over a certain age can vote in elections for their chosen political representatives, and so they have a say in how they are governed.

Although universal suffrage is now considered essential to a functioning democracy, this was not always the case. Until relatively recently, many countries had restrictions in place on who could vote. Barriers to voting have been based on gender, religion, race and ethnicity, land and property ownership, and the regions in which people lived.

CASE STUDY

The Chartists

Chartism was a British working-class movement that arose in 1838, at a time when voting was restricted to land- and property-owning elites. A key aim of the movement was to extend voting rights to all men. The Chartists organized mass protests and presented petitions to parliament. These petitions were rejected, and the movement failed to achieve its aims. However, fear of social unrest led the government to reform the voting laws several decades later.

First to vote
The emergence of democracy in the US and Western Europe initially led to voting rights being given to middle- and upper-class men who owned land or property.

Women get the vote
In the early 20th century, campaigns by women, such as the "suffragists" in the UK and the US (from the word "suffrage," meaning the right to vote), led many countries to adopt universal suffrage.

These restrictions ensured that political power remained in the hands of the most privileged.

Fighting for voting rights

Universal suffrage was won on several fronts. In the 18th and 19th centuries, working-class movements, such as Chartism (see opposite), campaigned to enable all men to vote, not just men from the upper classes. During the same period, movements to enable women to vote also gained momentum (see pp.130–31). In the 20th century, civil rights movements sought to ensure that all citizens, irrespective of their ethnic background, could vote in elections. In many former European colonies, the struggle for voting rights was tied to independence movements, and so countries such as India adopted universal suffrage on achieving independence.

Although many democracies now have universal suffrage, attempts to restrict voting among certain groups persist. This typically involves trying to make it harder for people from these groups to vote, sometimes by requiring them to carry forms of identification that they may not be able to afford.

Universal male suffrage
In the 19th and early 20th centuries, voting rights were extended to all adult males in most countries, irrespective of class, income, or whether or not they owned land or property.

"**Government does not rest upon force: it rests upon consent.**"
Emmeline Pankhurst, British political activist (1913)

Gaining the right to vote

The right to vote was won by different social groups at different times, often after long campaigns to have their voices heard. Such movements have been vital in overcoming voter restrictions based on wealth and class, on gender, and on race and ethnicity. Removing these restrictions began in the US and Western Europe at the end of the 19th century and continued throughout the 20th century.

VOTE

VOTE

Lifting race restrictions
Indigenous Australians gained voting rights in 1962, and racial discrimination in voting was outlawed in the US in 1965. In South Africa, Black people were prohibited from voting until 1994.

Women's rights

Over the past two centuries, people around the world have called for equal rights for women on issues such as access to education, voting, property ownership, and reproductive health.

The denial of rights

In the late 18th century, the issue of women's rights was beginning to receive public attention. According to the law in Britain at the time, a married woman had no right to own property or money, no right to vote, and no rights to her children. In 1792, English author Mary Wollstonecraft wrote *A Vindication of the Rights of Woman*—one of the earliest feminist works. In it, she argued that women deserved the same basic rights as men and that treating women as property undercut the moral foundation of society. Wollstonecraft's argument focused on education; she claimed that women were only seen as inferior to men because they did not have the same educational opportunities. Her book had a significant impact on advocates for women's rights in the 19th century and on the suffragist movement globally.

Writing around the same time in France, activist Olympe de Gouges (1748–1793) published *Declaration of the Rights of Woman and of the Female Citizen* (1791), asserting that women are equal to men and therefore entitled to the same rights. She was later executed for her beliefs.

Women's unequal rights

Inequalities between women and men can be seen in many aspects of social and political life, in both private and public spheres. This includes women who experience domestic violence, are denied the same education and job opportunities as men, and lack sufficient political representation. While movements for women's rights have brought progress, some inequalities do still persist.

The right to vote
Women were denied the right to vote in most countries until the early 20th century. There are still some countries where women find it difficult to vote.

The right to education
Women were denied the right to education in most societies until the 19th century. In some countries today, girls still have limited access to learning.

The right to own property
Until the 19th century, most women were not allowed to own property. Today, property laws in some countries still discriminate against women.

Struggle for rights

Progress was slow in the move toward rights for women. In Britain, it was not until 1870 that married women were legally allowed to keep the money that they earned and to own property. Across much of Europe and in North America, it was only after the suffragist movement in the early 20th century that women gained the right to vote.

The post–World War II era saw the emergence of the Women's Liberation Movement and the feminist movement (see pp.62–63), which led to a broader recognition of women's rights. As a result, the UN and other global agencies began to promote gender equality, and some nations changed their laws. However, the struggle continues in some countries, with women still being denied many of the same rights as men.

"Let us have the rights we deserve."

Alice Paul, suffragist who helped secure the vote for women in the US (c.1917)

ROLLING BACK WOMEN'S RIGHTS

While significant progress has been made on women's rights since the 1960s, there has been a growing backlash in recent years linked to the rise of right-wing populist governments around the world. There has been a focus on women's reproductive rights, with countries such as Poland introducing laws to make abortion illegal. This backwards step has also seen efforts to narrow the definition of domestic violence and sexual abuse and to block laws promoting equal pay.

Political representation
The first female head of state was elected in 1960 in Sri Lanka. Men still dominate politics, however, leading to laws and policies skewed against women.

Reproductive rights
Opposition to women's reproductive rights is common in certain societies—with some religions prohibiting family planning and abortion.

The right to equal pay
Since the 1950s, laws have been passed worldwide to secure equal pay for women. However, there are still differences in many nations.

The right to protection from domestic violence
Many women continue to face high levels of physical, emotional, and sexual abuse at home, despite most countries having laws against domestic violence.

Justice, identity, and inclusion

Justice refers to the notion that people get what they deserve. It is closely connected to identity and inclusion—injustice occurs when people are excluded because of their identity. American philosopher John Rawls (1921–2002) proposed an experiment known as the "veil of ignorance" in which people were asked to design a new society, without knowing their own position in it. He argued that because nobody would want to belong to a disadvantaged group, they would create a fair society.

Equality, equity, justice

The concepts of equality, equity, and justice can broadly be seen as ways of trying to address an underlying inequality. Inequality in this context refers to people having unequal access to resources and opportunities in societies—often because the system is devised in a way to privilege some and disadvantage others. One response is to promote equality—by distributing tools and assistance evenly across society. Another is to focus on equity, which recognizes that people have different needs and provides them with support. Justice focuses on addressing the underlying source of the inequality to promote a fair society in which people have equal access to resources and opportunities.

"Justice is the first virtue of social institutions, as truth is of systems of thought."

John Rawls, *A Theory of Justice* (1971)

Inequality

This arises when people have unequal access to resources and opportunities—some people can gain access, but others cannot without assistance, or even at all.

DIVERSITY AND INCLUSION

A common injustice is excluding people from opportunities because of their identity. There has been growing attention to promoting diversity and inclusion across society. Diversity acknowledges all the ways in which people are different, and inclusion ensures that everyone's thoughts and perspectives are valued. Promoting diversity and inclusion means empowering people by respecting and appreciating what makes them different, such as their age, gender, ethnicity, religion, disability, or sexual orientation. It involves a shift away from treating some identities as "normal", celebrating people's differences by ensuring equal access to opportunities for all.

85.8%
of Fortune 500 company CEOs are white males.

Richard Zweigenhaft, American writer, *Fortune 500 CEOs, 2000–2020: Still Male, Still White* (2020)

Equity
Recognizing that people have different needs, equity provides them with the necessary tools to ensure they can access resources and opportunities.

Justice
This refers to fixing the system to remove the source of the inequality so that everyone can gain access to resources and opportunities.

Classism

Discrimination based on social status, otherwise known as "classism," perpetuates inequalities in society and reduces the opportunities available for those from lower-class backgrounds.

Hierarchies

Social class refers to the hierarchical distinctions between individuals or groups in society. For much of human history, many societies existed with essentially two classes: those who owned land and those who worked for the landowners. In medieval Europe, this gave rise to manorialism (see below). More complex systems developed in other regions: India, for example, has one of the oldest class systems. This is based on lineage, with the priestly Brahman class, or caste, at the top; the Vaisya caste of artisans, farmers, and merchants in the middle; and a lower class of laborers. Below all of these are the "Dalits," who are restricted to occupations considered unclean by the religious establishment.

The term "social class" arose in 19th-century Europe, following the reorganization of society brought about by the Industrial Revolution. This period saw the emergence of a "middle class," who was able to indulge in the kinds of education and cultural activities once restricted to the landowners.

Discrimination

Classism is a form of discrimination based on treating people differently because of their social class. This discrimination can be individual and include unconscious bias. It can also be structural—a part of a system of policies and practices that are set up to benefit the upper classes at the expense of the lower classes. This might include a lack of access to the best schools and universities for those from the lower classes. This, in turn, limits employment opportunities, resulting in income inequalities.

Left-wing ideologies, such as socialism and communism, have traditionally focused on the need to eliminate class inequalities. Right-wing ideologies, such as conservatism, emphasize the need to maintain social order, which often tends to reinforce classism.

Middle class

The broadest of the three classes includes a range of low- to high-paid professionals, most of whom have earned a university degree.

Class structures

Most societies have some form of class structure. Generally, there are three social classes: an upper class of wealthy landowners or aristocrats, a middle class of professionals and business people, and a lower class of low-income workers.

 NEED TO KNOW

> **Manorialism** was a hierarchical system that flourished in medieval Europe. The "manor-owning" nobility owned the land and leased it to peasants in return for their labor.

> **The Industrial Revolution** of the 18th and 19th centuries transformed the agricultural societies of Europe and North America into mass-market industrial economies.

> **Social mobility** refers to the ability of people to move up in the social hierarchy.

Upper class

The upper class is the group at the top of the social hierarchy. In some societies, it includes anyone who has a substantial amount of wealth; in others, it consists only of people who are born into aristocratic families.

Social mobility

In socially mobile societies, people born into low-income families have opportunities to find well-paid jobs. In less socially mobile societies, a person's birth determines their path in life.

Lower class

People belonging to the lower class tend to be employed in low-paying jobs that offer little economic security.

Slavery

Slavery refers to the condition in which people are owned by others and denied basic rights and freedoms. Although it is now illegal, slavery still persists in many forms.

Legacy of suffering

Slavery is the ownership of one human being by another—a relationship in which the enslaved person is forced to do unpaid work for their enslaver. It has a long history and played a key role in building the empires of ancient Egypt, Greece, and Rome. It was common in Islamic societies from the time of the Prophet Muhammad onward and existed in many early kingdoms in Africa. Some enslaved people were prisoners of war or the offspring of enslaved people, while others had been kidnapped in slave raids or sold into servitude by families to settle debts.

However, slavery is most widely associated with the transatlantic slave trade that existed between the 16th and 19th centuries. During that time, between 10 and 12 million Black Africans were transported by European colonial powers to the Americas to work on plantations or in private households. When enslaved people arrived, the colonists, who included French, Portuguese, Spanish, British, Danish, and Dutch administrators, shipped sugar, tobacco, and other goods back to Europe. In return, they sold arms, textiles, and alcohol to people in their new colonies.

Those Black Africans forced into slavery faced horrific conditions, and many died during the journey to the Americas. The loss of so many people, together with the violence that accompanied slave raids, weakened African societies. Although slavery was abolished in the late 19th century, a major legacy has been the racism that people of African descent continue to face worldwide, particularly in multiracial countries.

METHODS OF CONTROL

Repeated violence, or the threat of violence.
Financial control, such as debt bondage or preventing access to money.
Emotional manipulation by making the victim feel responsible for their situation.
Control of drugs on which the victim may be made dependent.
Social isolation by restricting the victim's contact with others.

ABOLISHING SLAVERY

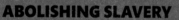

It took nearly 200 years for slavery to be abolished worldwide.

❭ **The transatlantic slave trade** was eventually brought to an end by a movement that began in the late 18th century, with Quakers questioning the morality of slavery.

❭ **The Haitian Revolution** (1791–1804) saw enslaved people overthrow their enslavers in the French colony, creating an independent state.

❭ **The American Civil War** (1861–1865) was fought when the Southern states moved to leave the Union because of the North's anti-slavery stance.

❭ **Slavery was prohibited in the US** in 1865 and abolished in Latin America in 1888. In 1948, slavery was outlawed in the Universal Declaration of Human Rights.

Modern slavery

Despite the abolition of slavery, there are millions around the world today trapped in what amounts to a modern form of slavery. This takes numerous forms, including unpaid labor, domestic servitude, and sexual exploitation. Perpetrators of modern slavery use various means to control and exploit their victims—who are often women and children.

EXPLOITATION OF LABOR

One of the most common forms of modern slavery involves forcing people to work for low or no wages, often in poor conditions.

DOMESTIC SERVITUDE

Trafficked people may be forced to work in private households as nannies or domestic help. They cannot leave, making this a form of enslavement.

HUMAN TRAFFICKING

Human trafficking refers to the use of force to exploit people for purposes such as prostitution, labor, criminality, marriage, or even organ removal.

40m
people are estimated to be trapped in a form of slavery.

www.antislavery.org, "What is modern slavery?"

CRIMINAL EXPLOITATION

Victimized people may be forced by criminal organizations to undertake illegal activities, such as drug dealing, shoplifting, or begging.

SEXUAL EXPLOITATION

Victims of all ages, genders, and sexual orientations can be forced, or coerced into providing sexual services and treated as commodities by criminals.

Racism and anti-racism

Racism is discrimination against people on the basis of their race or ethnicity. Anti-racism seeks to end racism and to ensure that people of all races and ethnicities are treated equally.

Inventing inequality

Racism is a form of tribalism that has existed in societies around the world for millennia. However, in recent centuries, it has become most associated with the period of European colonial rule, which lasted from the beginning of the 16th century until the mid-20th century (see pp.172–73). During that time, a host of European nations justified establishing colonies in Africa, Asia, Australia, and the Americas on the basis of the racist idea that white people were superior to the Indigenous people whom they subjugated. Although most of these colonies have since gained independence, notions of white supremacy still persist, and the histories of non-Western societies are often viewed through a European lens. Such histories tend to focus on the supposed improvements that Europeans made to those societies and ignore their pre-colonial pasts.

There are two principal forms of racism. Individual racism is a personal attitude of superiority that one person might have over another on the basis of their ethnicity. More pervasive is structural, or institutional, racism, whereby a society's institutions, such as its judicial system or police forces,

Structural racism

Structural, or institutional, racism is a form of prejudice that is embedded in social systems and is maintained by laws that are implemented by state authorities. For instance, in a white-dominated society, structures may deny basic rights and opportunities to people of color in a range of areas.

 UNFAIR PAY AND WORK PROSPECTS
Racism can affect people's salaries and career progression. People of color are often paid less than their white counterparts for doing the same work or may be overlooked for promotion.

 UNDERRESOURCED NEIGHBORHOODS
Structural racism can result in neighborhoods with residents of color receiving less investment than other neighborhoods. This perpetuates inequalities in housing, education, and health care.

DISCRIMINATION BY SOME EMPLOYERS
Even with the appropriate qualifications, people of color may find it hard to find employment due to racist prejudice by employers and remain underemployed or unemployed for this reason.

 ANTI-RACISM
The anti-racism movement is devoted to eradicating all forms of racism. In particular, it seeks to expose the ways in which social systems put racial and ethnic groups at a disadvantage.

 DISCRIMINATION BY LANDLORDS
Prejudiced landlords can prevent specific racial and ethnic groups from accessing housing. This can lead to the segregation of ethnic minorities into particular geographical areas.

 LIMITED EDUCATIONAL OPPORTUNITIES
Systemic racism in the education system can lead to children from particular racial and ethnic groups facing more limited education policies. This, in turn, can affect their opportunities in life.

are structured in ways that favor one ethnic group over another. Structural racism can involve the denial of basic rights to certain ethnic groups, such as when Black South Africans were segregated under the apartheid regime in the 20th century. It can also lead to genocide, as it did in Nazi Germany, when 6 million Jews, and many Slavic, Roma, and Sinti people, were killed in the Holocaust during World War II (see pp.46–47).

Fighting racism

Anti-racism is a movement that seeks to identify and oppose racism in all of its forms. It has its roots in the decolonization and civil rights movements of the 20th century and is inspired by thinkers such as W.E.B. Du Bois (1868–1963), Frantz Fanon (1925–1961), and Martin Luther King Jr. (1929–1968). One of its most recent manifestations is the Black Lives Matter movement (see box).

> "In a racist society, it is not enough to be non-racist... we must be anti-racist."
>
> Attributed to Angela Davis, American political activist (b. 1944)

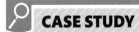

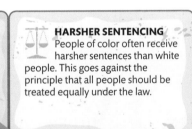

HARSHER SENTENCING
People of color often receive harsher sentences than white people. This goes against the principle that all people should be treated equally under the law.

RACISM IN HEALTH CARE
Studies show that people of color are impacted to a far greater extent by health issues than white people. They are also more likely to be misdiagnosed by health professionals and experience higher mortality rates.

UNFAIR LEGAL PROCESSES
Legal processes in some countries are often biased against particular racial and ethnic groups. This can occur throughout the legal system, including whether cases are heard in court, access to legal services, and court decisions.

POLICE VIOLENCE
In many countries, people of color are often subjected to disproportionate amounts of police violence. Statistically, they face a higher risk of being killed by police actions.

NEGATIVE MEDIA STEREOTYPING
People of color are often subjected to negative stereotyping by the media, from films to the news. This in turn fosters greater prejudice against these groups across society.

CRIMINALIZATION
People of color can face a greater risk of being targeted, profiled, fined, arrested, harassed, and incarcerated for minor offenses than white people.

RACIAL PROFILING
Due to racial profiling—suspecting individuals of criminal behavior based on their ethnicity—the police are more likely to stop and search a person of color than a white person. This undermines that person's civil liberties.

POLITICAL UNDER-REPRESENTATION
People of color are often poorly represented politically. This means that political processes may not meet their needs and may even perpetuate racist policies.

The patriarchy

Male-dominated societies are often referred to as patriarchal. Feminists have adopted the term *patriarchy* to refer to the social structures and practices that reinforce male domination and the oppression of women.

Women as the "Other"

Traditionally, the term *patriarchy* (from the Greek word for "rule of the father") has been used to describe a hierarchical political system in which men hold most of or all the power. Feminists have expanded this definition, applying it to the structures and power relations in society that serve to benefit men at the expense of women—at home, at work, and in culture, religion, and government.

The concept of the patriarchy rejects biological determinism. Instead, feminists argue that women are ascribed roles based not on biological differences but on attitudes and structures that view women as lesser beings. As French philosopher Simone de Beauvoir explained, men are seen as the norm in society and therefore as superior, while women are treated as the "Other" and hence as inferior.

Perpetuating patriarchy

Society tends to condition children to believe in male dominance from a young age, through expectations

Structures of oppression

The patriarchy, in feminist terms, refers to an interconnected set of structures—evident in institutions and practices at all levels of society—that enable men to oppress women. British sociologist Sylvia Walby (1953–) argues that the patriarchy operates through six such structures.

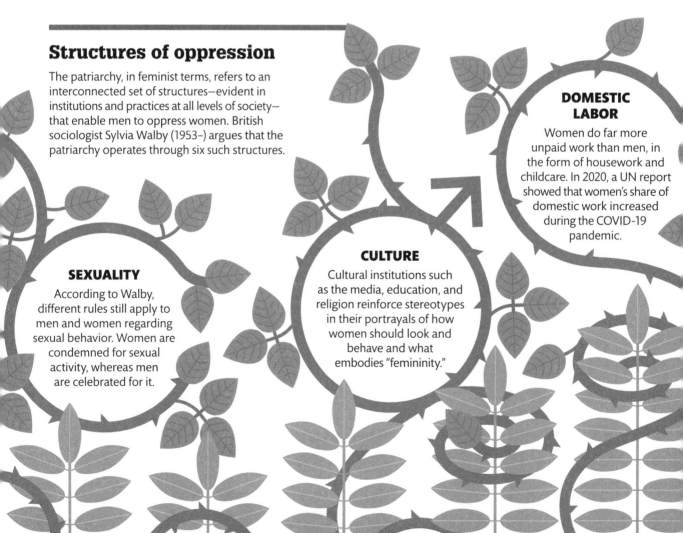

DOMESTIC LABOR
Women do far more unpaid work than men, in the form of housework and childcare. In 2020, a UN report showed that women's share of domestic work increased during the COVID-19 pandemic.

CULTURE
Cultural institutions such as the media, education, and religion reinforce stereotypes in their portrayals of how women should look and behave and what embodies "femininity."

SEXUALITY
According to Walby, different rules still apply to men and women regarding sexual behavior. Women are condemned for sexual activity, whereas men are celebrated for it.

of how girls and boys should behave and the jobs they should do, such as nursing or firefighting. Political and legal institutions reinforce these patriarchal views—from laws that favor men to those that undermine women's reproductive rights—as can religious practices and societal attitudes more broadly. Feminists argue that these serve to control women by setting norms of how they should behave, shaming those who do not conform, and that only by overturning such structures will women have equal opportunities.

A WORLD DESIGNED FOR MEN

In her book *Invisible Women: Exposing Data Bias in a World Designed for Men* (2019), British writer and feminist campaigner Caroline Criado Perez (1984–) shows how gender bias in data collection reproduces outcomes that privilege men and discriminate against women. Modern societies increasingly rely on data to make important decisions—yet much of these data fail to account for women. The gender data gap affects a range of areas, including government policy, workplaces, the media, and urban planning, and often results in laws, technologies, infrastructure, and even medical treatments that are biased. For example, women are 50 percent more likely to be misdiagnosed when having a heart attack: although men and women may experience different symptoms, those common among men are treated as typical.

VIOLENCE

Violence against women may not be random or individual; rather, it could be a systematic form of male control. Such violence remains pervasive around the world.

THE STATE

Many states inherently subdue women through policies and laws. Despite some gains—such as women being able to vote—politics continues to serve and be dominated by men.

PAID WORK

Women suffer from discriminatory pay and unfair treatment and do more part-time work than their male counterparts. They also often face poorer job security and opportunities.

"Peace in patriarchy is war against women."

Maria Miles, feminist scholar, *Patriarchy and Accumulation on a World Scale* (1986)

LGBTQ+ rights

Lesbian, gay, bisexual, transgender, and queer (LGBTQ+) movements exist to defend people who face discrimination because of their sexual orientation, gender identity, or gender expression.

The fight for LGBTQ+ rights

While many countries have included legislation protecting the rights of LGBTQ+ people, other nations have laws that discriminate against them. These range from not recognizing same-sex marriage to imposing the death penalty for performing homosexual acts.

Discrimination based on a person's sexual orientation, gender identity, and/or their gender expression has historically been linked to religious condemnation of homosexuality. In 1791, France, then in the process of revolution, became the first nation to decriminalize homosexuality, followed within five years by Monaco, the Kingdom of Prussia, Luxembourg, Belgium, and Brazil in 1830. The Ottoman Empire (predecessor of Turkey) decriminalized homosexuality in 1858, and in 1917, following the Russian Revolution, the Bolsheviks declared that "homosexual relationships and heterosexual relationships are treated exactly the same by the law." However, in 1933, Joseph Stalin recriminalized homosexual activity, with punishments of up to five years' hard labor.

The modern LGBTQ+ rights movement is widely considered to have begun with the 1969 "Stonewall riots." Throughout the 1960s, police in the US routinely raided and shut down gay bars. In response to a raid on New York's Stonewall Inn, members of the gay

Legal recognition

While homosexuality was legalized in France in 1791, in most countries it remained illegal well into the 20th century. Even today, many countries still have laws prohibiting homosexual relations.

Marriage equality

Marriage equality for same-sex couples was first legally recognized in the Netherlands in 2002. As of 2021, same-sex marriage is legally recognized in 29 countries.

PRIDE

Pride is a worldwide annual celebration of LGBTQ+ identity that takes place each summer. It commemorates the Stonewall riots and promotes the self-affirmation, equality, and increased visibility of LGBTQ+ people. Pride events are attended by millions globally, although they are met with opposition in many places. The worldwide symbol of LGBTQ+ Pride is the rainbow flag. The colors represent the diversity of the LGBTQ+ community.

LGBTQ+ parenting

As of 2021, it is legal for same-sex couples to adopt children in 27 countries. Many LGBTQ+ couples also have their own biological children.

community fought back when the police became violent. The event inspired a broader global movement seeking the decriminalization of homosexuality and the acceptance of same-sex partnerships in society, along with greater legal protections.

However, the rise of LGBTQ+ rights has been met with a backlash in many countries. This includes continued efforts to introduce repressive legislation that undermines LGBTQ+ rights.

Global LGBTQ+ rights

Despite more positive attitudes toward issues such as same-sex marriage and the rights of LGBTQ+ people, public opinion remains sharply divided by country and culture. Many LGBTQ+ people feel able to live more openly in areas such as Western Europe and the Americas than elsewhere but still face hate crimes in these places.

NEED TO KNOW

> **Lesbian** refers to a woman who has a romantic and/or sexual orientation toward women.

> **Gay** refers to a man who has a romantic and/or sexual orientation toward men; it can also be a generic term for lesbian and gay sexual orientation.

> **Bisexual** is a term used to describe a romantic and/or sexual orientation toward more than one gender.

> **Transgender** describes people whose sense of identity and gender does not correspond with their birth sex.

> **Queer** is an umbrella term for anyone who is non-heterosexual and/or whose sense of identity and gender does not correspond with their birth sex.

> **Plus (+)** signifies all the gender identities and sexual orientations that are not covered by "LGBTQ."

Anti-discrimination laws
Many countries have legal protections in place that prohibit any discrimination against people on the grounds of their sexual orientation or gender identity.

Further recognition
Many countries now legally recognize nonbinary or third gender classifications. Supporters argue that people should be able to define their gender in the way that suits them.

Public spaces
In North America and Western Europe, there is ongoing political debate over access to public toilets by gender or transgender identity as opposed to a person's birth sex.

"LGBT rights are human rights."
www.unfe.org (2021)

Intersectionality

The term *intersectionality* describes the ways in which race, class, gender, and other personal factors can combine to create different kinds of prejudice and privilege in society.

All inequality is not equal

Few people would dispute that some groups are more privileged than others in society. However, what is less understood are the ways in which people can be privileged or disadvantaged by such accidental characteristics as their gender, class, ethnicity, sexuality, age, and ability. For example, a white woman may be disadvantaged because of her gender, but a Black woman may be disadvantaged because of her gender and her race. Likewise, a Black lesbian might experience prejudice because of her ethnicity, her gender, and her sexual orientation. The ways in which such factors can create inequality is known as intersectionality.

The word *intersectional* was coined in 1989 by Black American legal scholar and specialist in race and gender issues Kimberlé Crenshaw. She argued that the experience of being a Black woman could not be understood in terms of being Black and being a woman independently of each other, but that the interactions between the two had to be considered.

Crenshaw drew attention to how Black women were treated in the US court system: they were viewed

Overlapping identities

Although the origins of intersectionality lie with issues specifically facing Black women, it has since become a framework for understanding how different aspects of an individual's social and political identity, far beyond their race and gender, can combine to create different forms of disadvantage and privilege.

Class

People may be discriminated against because of their social class (see pp.136–137). Typically, this prejudice is directed against those from disadvantaged backgrounds.

Religion

People from religious minorities may face prejudice from individuals as well as discriminatory laws and policies by the state.

Sexual orientation

The LGBTQ community still faces prejudice in many countries

KYRIARCHY

Where patriarchy (see pp.142–143) is the traditional male authority over women, kyriarchy (from the Greek *kyrios*, meaning "lord or master," and *archion*, meaning "rule") is a theory explaining how each of us, whatever our gender, has many privileges that we are able to abuse. In this sense, patriarchy is a subset of kyriarchy, as is heteronormativity, which privileges heterosexuality over homosexuality.

Kyriarchy relates to intersectionality because they are both concerned with examining overlapping systems of characteristics. However, kyriarchy is more concerned with how power is controlled through structures that privilege certain qualities (for example maleness, whiteness) and vilify and oppress those with other qualities (such as femaleness or Blackness).

Age

Many people are discriminated against because of their age. Such prejudice can be directed against a range of different age groups.

Ethnicity

People from ethnic minorities frequently face prejudice. This is often due to their language and culture, or the color of their skin, or other inherited characteristics.

Power and marginalization

Intersectionality looks at the multiple ways in which people can be privileged or disadvantaged. Understanding these factors enables governments to ensure that people who are disadvantaged are given better opportunities to participate on equal terms with everyone else in society.

Ability

People with disabilities are often treated as being inferior and may also be excluded from jobs that they are perfectly fit to perform.

Gender

Gender inequality persists around the world. There are still very many areas in which women are denied the same opportunities as men in society.

as facing either the same issues as white women with regard to their gender or the same issues as Black men with regard to their race. Crenshaw argued that in doing so, the courts ignored the challenges specific to Black women as a group.

Promoting inclusivity

Recognition of intersectionality has been particularly important for activism and social movements. It highlights the need for inclusivity and fairer representation. For example, the feminist agenda has traditionally been set by white female professionals; intersectional feminism means not focusing solely on breaking the glass ceiling for women professionals but on raising the minimum wage for poorer working women.
Intersectionality has faced a sharp backlash from many on the right of the political spectrum, who claim that it is divisive and perpetuates a victim mentality. However, proponents argue that intersectionality sheds greater light on the ways in which people are either privileged or discriminated against, depending on their particular identities.

"All forms of marginalization intersect with and exacerbate one another."

Julia Serano, American trans activist, "Leftist Critiques of Identity Politics," *Medium* (2018)

Pressure groups and protest

For some citizens, voting is their only involvement in the political process. Others, however, want a deeper engagement and might be looking to influence some particular actions or policies of their government. These people might work as part of a pressure group or become involved in direct protests. Both of these activities are ways that people can participate in the political process without having to join a political party.

How pressure groups operate

A pressure group is an association of individuals who are united by a common political cause. The aim is literally to put pressure on governments to implement particular policies. The group applies this pressure from outside rather than seeking political power. Tactics can include lobbying officials, building public support, and mobilizing protests, which may be peaceful or involve civil disobedience. Some of what are known as "insider groups" regularly consult with governments; others, known as "outsider groups," have no official influence and may be radical.

Campaigning

In order to achieve their goals, pressure groups typically create and distribute promotional material, fund-raise, buy advertising space, make use of social media, and organize public meetings.

Endorsing candidates

Pressure groups do not seek to enter government but may endorse a political candidate who supports their cause on the basis that, if elected, they will promote that cause while in office.

Informing the public

It is necessary for pressure groups to raise public awareness of their particular cause, or causes, and gain public support. This is an important pillar of any campaign.

"Never doubt a small group of thoughtful, committed citizens can change the world; indeed, it is the only thing that ever has."

Attributed to Margaret Mead, British anthropologist

TYPES OF PRESSURE GROUPS

Interest groups

Pressure groups sometimes exist within organizations, such as trade unions, in which membership is restricted by profession. Known as "interest groups," these associations advocate on behalf of their members and do their best to draw attention to their particular concerns.

Cause groups

Some groups campaign on specific causes. These range from human, Indigenous, and disability rights through to campaigners against the arms trade or to help the environment. They champion causes, issues, or ideas that may not be of direct benefit to group members.

Demonstrating

Public demonstrations are a way of raising awareness, whether that is a small group holding placards in a town center or some form of direct action, such as blockades, sit-downs, or strikes.

Petitioning

Petitions are an important tool that can demonstrate the extent of public support for a cause. Petitions, traditionally on paper, now commonly online, are then presented to elected representatives.

Lobbying

Lobbying can be an effective means of influencing politicians (see pp.150–51). This may involve writing letters or arranging meetings with elected representatives.

Lobbying

Lobbying is a process by which members of the public, whether as private individuals or as representatives of organizations, try to persuade elected politicians to support their views in government.

Applying pressure

Lobbying, or exerting influence over governments, is not a new phenomenon. Taking its name from the hallways, or lobbies, in the UK's Houses of Parliament, where constituents gather to see their Member of Parliament (MP), lobbying is an essential part of the democratic process. In theory, it is a positive thing, in so far as it enables people to inform MPs about their concerns and provide them with valuable information (see pp.148–49). However, it can also be a means by which powerful interest groups can influence politicians at the expense of the public interest. For example, in 2016, following intensive lobbying by the plastics industry, targets for plastic recycling were cut by the UK government by nearly 10 percent. Although corporations can influence governments in this way perfectly legally, they may also do so in questionable ways, such as by paying politicians to adopt and fight for their causes, rewarding them either directly in cash or with offers of well-paid work.

The lobbying procedure

Individuals or groups may lobby politicians, although larger groups may hire professional lobbyists to work on their behalf. Individuals or smaller groups may arrange personal meetings with legislators.

Think tanks

Pressure groups often employ teams of experts, or "think tanks," to gather information and provide advice on how to influence politicians.

Interest groups

Lobbying, which usually involves face-to-face meetings, is done by many different interest groups and individuals. It may be done by political groups, such as Greenpeace, or by special-interest groups within the private, corporate sector.

Lobbyist

If a pressure group has enough money, it may employ a professional lobbyist to speak to politicians and advocate on its behalf.

A lucrative business

Lobbying is seen as an integral part of modern participatory government but is only legally regulated in a few countries. For example, in the US, it is protected by the First Amendment, which guarantees that members of the public have the right "to petition the government for a redress of grievances." Worldwide, there are growing demands for stricter government guidelines about lobbying practices, not least because lobbying has now become a global, and very powerful, multi-billion-dollar business.

THE REVOLVING DOOR

In a process known as the "revolving door," many politicians leave political office to become professional lobbyists for the corporations they helped when they were in government. Doing so helps those corporations maintain their ability to influence political decisions. It is a highly controversial practice, and so, in many countries, it is illegal for politicians to become lobbyists right after stepping down from their government roles.

Direct techniques

Lobbyists communicate directly with legislators, ministers, government officials, or anyone connected with passing legislation. In doing so, they try to influence the government's decision-making processes.

RESEARCH
Lobbyists often use think tanks to do research, which enables them to make informed pitches to legislators.

FUNDING
Powerful interest groups may offer donations or gifts to political parties, lawmakers, or candidates running for office.

THREATS
Lobbyists may even threaten legislators by pointing to the downside of not supporting their cause.

Indirect techniques

Sometimes known as "grassroots" lobbying, pressure groups often do not use professional lobbyists but aim to get public support for their causes by holding public meetings.

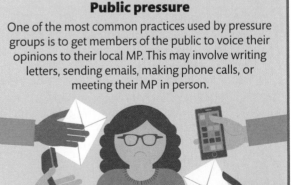

Public pressure

One of the most common practices used by pressure groups is to get members of the public to voice their opinions to their local MP. This may involve writing letters, sending emails, making phone calls, or meeting their MP in person.

Trade unions

Formed by associations of workers who come together to achieve common goals, such as better wages and working conditions, trade unions can also wield significant political power.

The role of the union

Trade, or labor, unions are membership-based organizations that bring together workers in the same industry or profession. A trade union typically consists of a subscription-paying membership, paid staff, and officers, including an elected general secretary who is often the public face of the union.

The union's primary function is to achieve the best possible conditions of employment for its members; this may include wages, sick and holiday pay, health and safety, and hours of work. It does this by negotiating with employers or management in a process that is known as "collective bargaining"—in other words, union representatives are empowered to speak on behalf of all unionized workers.

If all else fails, unions have one powerful tool: they can instruct members to strike. In addition to bargaining with employers, trade unions also provide benefits for members, such as hardship funds and legal advice.

Solidarity

The modern trade union emerged in the UK during the late 18th century, when industrialization created a new class of workers, which Karl Marx called the proletariat (see pp.54–55). Unions appeared in other industrializing nations, notably the US, Germany, Poland, and France. Today, Denmark, Sweden, and Finland have the most unionized workforces.

Trade unions are, by definition, political, not least because they unite workers. One of the UK's two main political parties, the Labour Party, grew out of the trade union movement. In Poland, union leader Lech Walesa successfully challenged the Polish Communist Party and was elected president in 1990. France may have the smallest unionized workforce of any EU nation (less than 8 percent of the workforce), but union action regularly brings the country to a standstill—as seen in 2019–2020, when there were strikes over proposed pension reforms. However, unions are currently facing challenges from globalization, zero-hour contracts, and changing economic and social conditions.

INDUSTRIAL ACTION

A trade union's most powerful weapon is to strike, or slow down labor.

 Economic strike Employees stop work to demand improvements to their economic well-being, such as increased wages and better vacation and sick leave.

 Sympathy strike A form of solidarity in which one union, which may not be in dispute, goes on strike to support another union that is already on strike.

 General strike Workers of all occupations go out on strike, with the aim of disrupting a whole community or entire country.

 Work to rule Union employees adhere strictly to contracted hours and conditions and refuse overtime in order to slow down production.

 Sick-out An organized number of workers calls in sick in order to disrupt work. This is used by police unions, whose members are not allowed to strike.

Collective bargaining

Based on the idea that people achieve more together than individually, collective bargaining is the process by which a group of workers "collectively" negotiate with an employer via trade union representatives speaking on behalf of members. Negotiations may include "red lines," which are conditions that, if not met, invalidate the negotiations. A collective agreement is binding on both parties. However, collective bargaining can only happen if the employer formally recognizes the union.

NEGOTIATING EMPLOYEE RIGHTS

Wages and benefits
Negotiations frequently center on wages, particularly annual raises, as well as bonuses and benefits. Wage bargaining can be tough, especially in a poor economic climate.

Working conditions
Any changes to employees' working conditions, such as changes to contracts or to health and safety regulations, are also negotiated through the union.

Employer
Provided the union is officially recognized, the employer must conduct all negotiations regarding employee rights through that union.

Other issues
Union representatives also negotiate over other non-pay-related issues, such as working hours, layoffs, holidays, and flexible working hours for parents and caregivers.

Breakdown
If collective bargaining breaks down, unions may seek arbitration or some sort of mediation. Alternatively, and as a last resort, a trade union will call for strike action.

NEGOTIATION

General secretary
Unions are hierarchical and overseen by a general secretary who is elected by the members.

Representatives
Most unions have a negotiation committee whose representatives meet with employers.

COMMUNICATION

Other unions
Almost every profession has its own union. Each negotiates for its own members. However, union delegates come together in congresses to discuss issues that affect all workers.

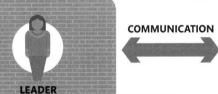

LEADER

REPRESENTATIVES

Members
Members' subscriptions are used to fund the union's activities and its paid staff.

Nonmembers
Nonmembers do not receive benefits but are included in the terms of collective agreements.

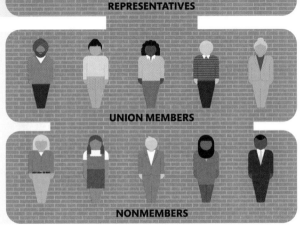

UNION MEMBERS

NONMEMBERS

> "The essence of trade unionism is social uplift."

A. Philip Randolph, American labor leader and civil rights activist, Washington march speech (1963)

Activism and protest

Social and political changes do not just happen—they are hard-won. People fight for their rights, which means getting politically active and protesting to highlight injustice and force change.

Taking a stand

Activism and protests often erupt when governments or those in power refuse to accept the need for change. Activists may act alone, as in Swedish environmentalist Greta Thunberg's school strike in 2018, which spiraled into a global protest by children against climate change in 2019, or collectively, as in the Black Lives Matter movement (pp.140–141), which went global following the murder of George Floyd in the US in 2020.

The fight for human rights and resentment of authoritarian rule have been the drivers for most protests. Significant 20th-century movements include women's fight for the vote, the civil rights movement, the pro-democracy Tiananmen Square protests in

Petitions and letters

Written protests in the form of petitions or letters to the press or politicians allow activists to raise awareness of an issue from home.

Social media

Increasingly popular, social media activism enables people to debate issues online. Hashtag campaigns often reach a wide audience.

Types of action

The aim of protest movements is to publicize issues, win support, and encourage or force legislators to make positive changes. While some activists resort to destructive, illegal means, most movements favor nonviolent direct action—a form of civil disobedience designed to interrupt daily life and gain as much publicity as possible without causing harm. The nonviolent direct action taken by Extinction Rebellion in its bid to highlight the climate crisis includes demonstrations and dramatic sit-ins.

Boycotts

Refusing to buy or use products or services can be effective because it disrupts a country's economy. A decades-long boycott of South African goods worldwide helped end apartheid in 1994.

China in 1989, and the protests across Eastern Europe, also in 1989, that led to the fall of the Berlin Wall and the collapse of many communist regimes. More recent anti-government protests include the Arab Spring of 2010–2012.

Right to protest

Activism is often perceived as left wing, but this is not always the case; many of the protests during the COVID-19 pandemic were driven by right-wing concerns about liberty. Governments also deal with activism in different ways. In most democracies, the state tolerates some right of protest, although there are usually limits, and many protests end in arrests. More authoritarian regimes discourage protest and respond harshly.

> "We are here, not because we are law-breakers; we are here in our efforts to become law-makers."
>
> Emmeline Pankhurst, British political activist, "Speech from the Dock" (1908)

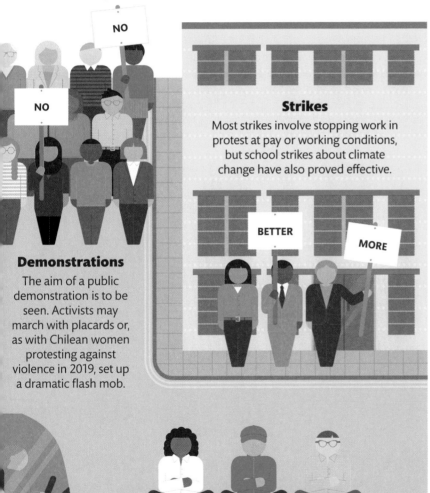

Demonstrations
The aim of a public demonstration is to be seen. Activists may march with placards or, as with Chilean women protesting against violence in 2019, set up a dramatic flash mob.

Strikes
Most strikes involve stopping work in protest at pay or working conditions, but school strikes about climate change have also proved effective.

Sit-ins
A powerful form of protest is to refuse to move. In 1960, four Black students sat at a Woolworth's lunch counter in Greensboro, North Carolina, to protest its whites-only service. Six months later, the store changed the policy.

THE #METOO MOVEMENT

Women have protested against abuse by men for decades. One of the most successful campaigns was the #MeToo movement against sexual harassment and the abuse of women. The movement began in the US in 2006 when survivor and activist Tarana Burke began using the phrase "me too" to encourage other women to come forward with their accounts of sexual abuse, particularly at work. In 2017, allegations of sexual abuse were made against former film producer Harvey Weinstein, and the movement went viral as a hashtag campaign, with women all over the world sharing their experiences and accusing many powerful men of wrongdoing.

Revolutions

In a democracy, citizens can remove an unpopular government with an election. But when an authoritarian regime hangs on to power against the will of most people, discontent may lead to revolution.

Demand for change

There are many different kinds of revolution—political, economic, social, religious, and cultural—but common to all is the replacement of an existing system with a new one. Revolutions demand radical change and, in terms of sociopolitical revolutions, this may mean using force to replace an unyielding regime.

The 18th and 19th centuries saw a wave of revolutions, kick-started by the American Revolution (1765–1791). American colonists rebelled against British rule and achieved independence, resulting in the establishment of the United States. Influenced by this, but fueled also by economic hardship and a rigid monarchy, the French Revolution (1789–1799) led to the

creation of a republic. Both inspired further revolutions across Europe in 1848 against monarchies.

The workers revolt

In 1917, revolution swept across Russia. Inspired by Marxism, the Bolsheviks overthrew the imperial dynasty and established the world's first communist state (see pp.54–55). Other countries,

Causes of revolutions

Revolutions can be triggered by a combination of factors, including poverty, oppression, a lack of rights, and the refusal of a ruling elite to enact change. Usually, social tensions and discontent have been building for years.

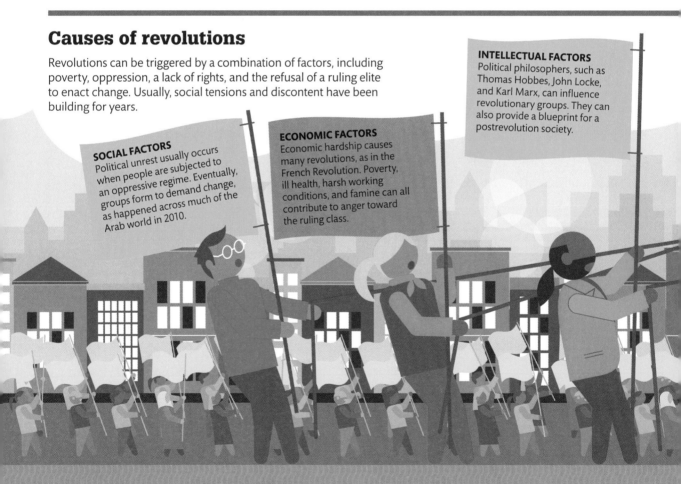

INTELLECTUAL FACTORS
Political philosophers, such as Thomas Hobbes, John Locke, and Karl Marx, can influence revolutionary groups. They can also provide a blueprint for a postrevolution society.

SOCIAL FACTORS
Political unrest usually occurs when people are subjected to an oppressive regime. Eventually, groups form to demand change, as happened across much of the Arab world in 2010.

ECONOMIC FACTORS
Economic hardship causes many revolutions, as in the French Revolution. Poverty, ill health, harsh working conditions, and famine can all contribute to anger toward the ruling class.

notably China and Cuba, followed suit. But revolutions do not guarantee the desired outcome. For instance, in the Soviet Union, attempts to impose communism led to famine, hardship, and violence. Led by Joseph Stalin, the country became a one-party dictatorship (see pp.76–77) rather than a workers' state.

While many revolutions involve force and considerable bloodshed, this is not always the case; change can be achieved by nonviolent means. In 2001, Philippine activists peacefully toppled their president, Joseph Estrada, and in 2004, the Orange Revolution (a series of mass protests in Ukraine) peacefully overturned a corrupt election result.

> ## "No real social change **has ever come about** without a revolution."
>
> Emma Goldman, American anarchist, *Anarchism and Other Essays* (1910)

✓ NEED TO KNOW

> **A coup d'état** is the sudden, violent seizure of power by a small group, often the military.

> **The Enlightenment** was a 17th- and 18th-century intellectual movement that promoted ideas of freedom, liberty, fraternity, and separation of church and state.

> **Marxism** is a socioeconomic analysis of capitalism, put forward by German philosopher Karl Marx, who advocated for a workers' revolution (see pp.52–55).

POLITICAL FACTORS
The aim of most revolutions is to liberate a population from an oppressive regime, whether it is domestic or foreign. Critical tipping points may arise when the population can no longer tolerate its rights being violated.

TIPPING POINTS
Revolutions occur when other means of making changes have failed. The tipping point may be simple—such as Russia women demanding bread in 1917, which sparked the Russian Revolution.

A new government
Most revolutions seek to destroy and replace an existing regime. The new government usually includes leaders of the revolution or individuals chosen by them.

INTERNATIONAL RELATIONS

International connections

A key responsibility of government is to protect its citizens and to defend its country's borders. However, it must also ensure that its borders are open for international trade and that it maintains diplomatic relations with other countries. To do this, governments across the world regularly sign political treaties with each other and make trade agreements that protect their individual interests.

International borders

International borders vary significantly, from highly contested ones—such as those that divide a culturally united population—to borders that have long been accepted as natural dividing lines between culturally distinct peoples. In general, there are three types of international borders.

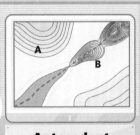

Antecedent border

This is a border that is laid down in an unpopulated area before any clear settlements have appeared there.

Subsequent border

This is a border that is laid down after that area has been settled and become home to people of a particular culture.

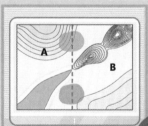

Superimposed border

This is an artificial border created by external powers with little regard for local populations, such as by European nations when colonizing Africa.

MARITIME BORDERS

All of Earth's landmasses are surrounded by water, which acts as a natural political border for many countries. However, not all coastlines are the same, and it is not always easy to judge exactly where the land meets the sea. For this reason, the United Nations Convention on the Law of the Sea states that a maritime boundary lies 12 nautical miles (22 km) out into the sea from a baseline judged to be the edge of a country's coast. Beyond these territorial waters lies an Exclusive Economic Zone, which stretches 200 nautical miles (370 km) out to sea and gives a country the right to exploit the sea and the seabed in that area. Beyond this zone lie international waters, which are subject to international law.

"In the 21st century, we are defined not by our borders, but by our bonds."

Barack Obama, 44th president (2010)

Border regulations

In recent decades, borders have become both increasingly regulated, such as in areas that have experienced rises in migration, and less regulated, such as between countries that have signed legally recognized regional cooperation treaties.

Open border

An open border, such as those among EU member states, enables people to move freely between countries, with few restrictions.

Regulated border

A regulated border, such as that between the US and Mexico, imposes different degrees of control on the movement of people and goods.

Demilitarized border

A demilitarized border creates a zone in which warring powers agree to cease military activity—for example between North and South Korea.

Diplomacy

Diplomats have always played a vital role in international relations. Their purpose is to influence the decisions of foreign governments through a combination of negotiation and nonviolent persuasion.

Early diplomats

In premodern times, diplomacy was largely concerned with relationships between neighbors and had little to do with setting up permanent bases for ambassadors abroad. However, diplomats were always needed to represent their governments, whether to make trade agreements, to secure allies, or to avert conflict. Generally, they were members of the aristocracy who were close to their ruler and who could help finance the journeys they had to make.

The Roman Catholic Church provided one of the first modern models of diplomacy—one that relied on an elaborate legal system as well as a large institutional framework that brought church councils together from around the world. The early Italian city-states, such as Venice and Genoa, also laid the groundwork for modern diplomacy by establishing the first resident envoys. The most famous of these was the Florentine scholar Niccolò Machiavelli (see pp.26–27).

Foreign policy

The professionalization of diplomacy went hand in hand with the increasing specialization of government departments. In 1626, Cardinal Richelieu (1585–1642) established the first modern foreign ministry in France. He recognized that diplomacy was one of the most important tools of government and that it had to be aligned with state policy priorities, both at home and abroad.

Due to the enormous cost of waging war, diplomacy was transformed during the early modern period, becoming more focused on maintaining peace and minimizing the effects of ongoing conflict. The first European peace conferences tried to provide lasting frameworks for political stability by encouraging powerful states to work and govern together. The Concert of Europe, which formed in 1814, laid the groundwork for the current international system, which relies heavily on international institutions to manage political issues that concern all the major powers.

> **"Successful diplomacy is an alignment of objectives and means."**
>
> Attributed to Dennis Ross, US diplomat

Reaching out

Diplomats are most urgently needed when two or more states come into conflict. For this reason, diplomats are given diplomatic immunity when they are working abroad. This guarantees that they cannot be arrested and that their belongings cannot be seized.

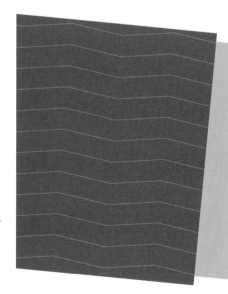

✓ NEED TO KNOW

> **Preventative diplomacy** seeks to contain international crises. Pioneered by the United Nations, it was used by Secretary-General U Thant when he intervened in the Cuban Missile Crisis in 1962.

> **Bilateral negotiations** involve two parties. They are often used to level expectations, obtain concessions, and maintain commitment.

> **Accords** are formal agreements between states.

The diplomatic service

The body of diplomats and foreign policy officers employed by a government is known as its diplomatic service. Its role is to communicate with the governments of other countries.

Embassies

Permanent diplomatic missions to foreign countries are housed in embassies. These also serve as places where the guest state's citizens can be protected, if necessary, from the host state.

Treaties

Successful negotiations can end in a treaty, which is binding under international law; a convention, which is less formal; or a protocol, which prolongs, amends, or supersedes an existing agreement.

Sanctions

If states fail to agree on important issues, one state may impose sanctions on another. These can include economic and trade sanctions, arms embargoes, travel bans, and financial or commodity restrictions.

CASE STUDY

The Iran nuclear deal

In 2015, Iran signed a landmark agreement, known as the Joint Comprehensive Plan of Action (JCPOA), with several world powers, under which it promised to dismantle its nuclear research program. In return, the international community lifted sanctions it had imposed on Iran to prevent it from developing nuclear weapons, which were costing the country billions of dollars in lost revenue. The negotiations involved the EU, the US, and six other countries and took two years to complete.

Global international organizations

Global international organizations are political bodies that include members from more than one nation. They aim to bring states together to address global issues and work toward common goals.

Global issues

Historically, international political organizations, such as the League of Nations, provided platforms for states to express their priorities to a global audience, with the aim of reaching shared goals. Due to globalization and the spread of global crises, such as the COVID-19 pandemic and climate change, states now have to consider not only their own priorities but also those of the world at large. For this reason, the international organizations of today often have a "voice" and identity of their own, sometimes acting independently of the interests of their member states. The most powerful of these is the United Nations (UN), established in 1945 (see box), which aims to avoid, or resolve, conflicts between states through non-violent, diplomatic means. As of 2021, the UN has 193 member states (as well as two observer states—Palestine and the Holy See).

In addition to its main departments, such as the UN General Assembly and the UN Security Council, the UN also works with

The UN and related organizations

The UN is perhaps the most recognized global international organization. It works with a range of specialized international organizations to tackle issues such as global security, international justice, human rights, health, climate change, migration, and food and water security.

International Monetary Fund (IMF)

The IMF fosters economic growth by providing financial assistance to lower-income countries. It currently has $28 billion in outstanding loans to 74 states.

97m

people in 88 countries were given food and assistance by the UN in 2020.

UN Department of Global Communications (2021)

World Bank

The World Bank works in more than 100 countries. It provides low-interest loans, interest-free credit, and grants to poorer countries for education, health, and infrastructure development.

15 specialized agencies to achieve its aims, overseeing several major global organizations (see below). The goal of these and other organizations is to provide rules that enable states to trade and communicate more effectively, and to help avert humanitarian disasters caused by pandemics, wars, and climate change.

FOUNDATION OF THE UNITED NATIONS

The UN was formed in 1945 to improve international co-operation following World War II (1939–45), and was a successor to the League of Nations. Fifty governments took part in the San Francisco conference that drafted the UN Charter and set out the UN's original objectives, which included maintaining international peace and security, developing friendly relations among nations, and promoting social progress, better living standards, and human rights.

THE UN

In addition to its main bodies (the General Assembly, the Security Council, the Economic and Social Council, the Trusteeship Council, the International Court of Justice, and the Secretariat), the UN oversees several major global international organizations.

World Health Organization (WHO)

The WHO is committed to improving the health of people in all nations to the highest possible level. It defines health as a state of complete well-being rather than merely the absence of disease.

International Atomic Energy Agency (IAEA)

The IAEA is the world's center for cooperation in the field of nuclear technology. Working with multiple partners, the agency ensures that nuclear technologies are used safely.

Food and Agriculture Organization (FAO)

The FAO leads international efforts to fight hunger. One of its many roles is to help broker trading agreements between lower- and higher-income countries.

Intergovernmental organizations

For sovereign nations, membership in an intergovernmental organization (IGO) can bring a variety of benefits, from favorable trade agreements to military support.

Strength through unity

IGOs bring together two or more independent nation-states into a single entity to work together on issues of common interest. An IGO is formalized by all its members signing a treaty, which gives the organization legal status, distinguishing it from other, more informal economic or political gatherings. The treaty binds all of its signatories to a single jurisdiction (a system of law courts) that transcends the power of national courts and enables disputes to

Trading blocs

IGOs are often formed to help reduce or eliminate barriers to trade among participating states. They can take the form of preferential trading areas that focus on particular products; free-trade areas with a common external tariff; common markets that secure freedom of movement of capital, labor, and goods and services; and economic and monetary unions (see box below). Each trading bloc offers different degrees of economic and political integration.

CASE STUDY

The euro

The introduction of the European currency, the euro, on New Year's Day, 1999, was the largest monetary changeover in history. The currency was adopted by 12 EU member states at first but is now the official currency of 19 of the 27 nations in the EU. There are now over 1.3 trillion euros in circulation. It is the second-largest reserve currency as well as the world's second-most traded currency after the US dollar.

European Union (EU)

The EU is an economic and political union of 27 member states, primarily located in Europe. It has an internal single market with a standardized system of laws that apply to all members.

United States-Mexico-Canada Agreement (USMCA)

Signed into law in 2020 to replace the 1994 North America Free Trade Agreement (NAFTA), the USMCA is a trilateral trade-bloc agreement between the US, Mexico, and Canada.

Caribbean Community (CARICOM)

Established in 1973, CARICOM promotes economic integration and cooperation between its 15 member states, which are relatively small in terms of population and economic output and face similar challenges.

Southern Common Market (MERCOSUR)

MERCOSUR is South America's largest trading bloc, made up of Argentina, Paraguay, Brazil, and Uruguay. Venezuela was suspended in 2016 for human rights violations.

African Union (AU)

The AU was founded in 2001 to replace the Organization of African Unity. Its 55 member states meet twice a year to promote sustainable growth, unity, and cooperation.

be settled and new agreements made. Strong IGOs are able to act with almost statelike authority. One obvious benefit of forming such a bloc is economic: together, an IGO's member states represent a more powerful manufacturing base and an enlarged consumer market, which gives the organization increased leverage when it comes to negotiating trade agreements with third parties.

Beyond economics

IGOs serve many purposes beyond trade and vary in size and scope, from global international organizations, such as the UN (see pp.164–65) or the more specialized International Criminal Police Organization (INTERPOL), which enables its 194 member states to share data on crimes and criminals, to IGOs that serve the interests of a particular region or focus on a specific issue. The North Atlantic Treaty Organization (NATO), for example, is dedicated to regional defense. Not all IGOs base their membership criteria on geography, however: only oil-producing countries can join the Organization of the Petroleum Exporting Countries (OPEC).

All this comes at a cost: notably, a willingness to surrender some degree of sovereignty and abide by the priorities of the IGO as a whole.

Eurasian Economic Union (EEU)

Founded in 2014, the EEU unites Armenia, Belarus, Kazakhstan, Kyrgyzstan, and Russia in a free-trading, integrated single market of 180 million people.

South Asian Association for Regional Cooperation (SAARC)

SAARC is a geopolitical union of eight South Asian states, including India and Pakistan, and nine observer states. It covers 21 percent of the world's population.

Association of Southeast Asian Nations (ASEAN)

ASEAN's 10 members include some of the world's fastest growing economies, but the organization also facilitates political, military, and social integration.

Arab League

Formed in 1945 to promote political stability and economic growth, the league has grown from six to 22 members, almost all from Africa and the Middle East.

Pacific Islands Forum (PIF)

The PIF aims to enhance the economic and social well-being of the people of the South Pacific by fostering cooperation between the governments of its 18 member states.

Foreign debt

Money borrowed by a government from creditors outside the country is known as foreign debt. It can provide much-needed short-term economic relief, but it also comes with risks.

Borrowing from abroad

Governments often need to raise money by borrowing from another country or from an international lender, such as a commercial bank or a global financial institution like the International Monetary Fund (IMF), World Bank (WB), or Asian Development Bank (ADB). There can be a variety of reasons for the need to take an external loan: for example, local debt markets may not be capable of meeting the state's financing needs, especially in emerging economies. Foreign lenders may also offer more competitive rates and more flexible periods of repayment.

Managed wisely, foreign debt can improve the standard of living in a country. It can allow the state to invest in infrastructure, such as new ports or roads, or to improve essential services like education. It can also boost economic growth.

The ability of countries to borrow from external lenders has helped finance growth and development not just in developing countries but in richer nations too. The US, for example, has the largest foreign debt of any country, currently valued at more than $22 trillion, and it is followed by the UK, France, Germany, and Japan.

Sustainable debt

A high amount of foreign debt is not necessarily a problem. Countries often maintain a level of foreign debt that is considered "sustainable" if the government is able to meet all its current and future repayment obligations.

LENDING AS A POLITICAL TOOL

In 2017, China became the world's largest official creditor, surpassing the World Bank and the IMF. A significant portion of this lending has been in support of China's Belt and Road Initiative (BRI). This is a strategy adopted by the Chinese in 2013 to invest in around 70 countries and international organizations. Money has been lent to countries to invest in roads, railways, and other infrastructure, and it is meant to stimulate economic growth. In response, the G7 countries, led by the US, launched their own Build Back Better World in 2021 to counter the influence of the Chinese BRI project.

Sources of global lending

The World Bank has traditionally been the main global lender. It is not a bank but an international organization that exists to provide cheap loans to developing countries to fund large infrastructure projects, so that these countries can tackle poverty and inequality. The IMF is a body that provides loans to member countries (of which there are 90) experiencing problems paying off their foreign debt.

Bilateral creditors

This is when one country lends to another. China is currently the major international bilateral creditor.

Multilateral creditors

Multilaterals are organizations with global memberships that promote economic growth—the World Bank, for example.

Commercial creditors

These include corporations, banks, and individuals who lend on commercial terms determined by market forces.

Terms and conditions

Multilateral and bilateral creditors typically offer tied loans, meaning that the funds have to be used for a predefined purpose or are linked to the implementation of a set of particular policies. Commercial creditors will typically make no such demands.

The most common figure used to assess the extent of a government's debt is its total debt as a proportion of gross domestic product (GDP).

Unsustainable debt

Problems arise when debt as a proportion of the GDP becomes too high. This happened in the Latin American Debt Crisis of the 1980s, when several countries in the region reached a point where foreign debt exceeded earning power. Incomes dropped, unemployment rose, and the banking system almost collapsed. The countries turned to the IMF, which lent money in exchange for economic reforms that favored free-market capitalism.

While borrowing is a viable source of funding, the IMF encourages countries to spend public funding efficiently, reduce corruption, and improve the overall business environment.

$19.5tn
was added to the global debt by the COVID-19 pandemic.

Bloomberg (2021)

International trade barriers

Governments use trade barriers to impose restrictions on international trade, with a view to protecting domestic industry, boosting their tax revenue, or reprimanding or retaliating against other states.

Protecting domestic interests

Trade barriers, such as tariffs, are a form of state interference in international trade. All governments rely on such interference to some degree and generally seek to discourage imports and encourage exports. Imposing tariffs on imported goods, for example, may prevent similar domestic products from being undercut. Likewise, quotas and state subsidies (see below) are designed to encourage local production. Another approach is to restrict or prohibit foreign investment in domestic plants and equipment. But such "protectionist" measures do not always have the desired effect. Foreign companies barred from a market by tariffs or quotas can often sidestep them by setting up a manufacturing plant in that country.

Many less economically developed nations rely on tariffs to supplement government tax revenues that would otherwise be harder to collect. They may also

Types of trade barrier

Different types of barrier can be imposed to limit the flow of goods into and out of a country. These include tariffs, which often lead to higher prices for consumers, and nontariff barriers, such as quotas or voluntary export restraints.

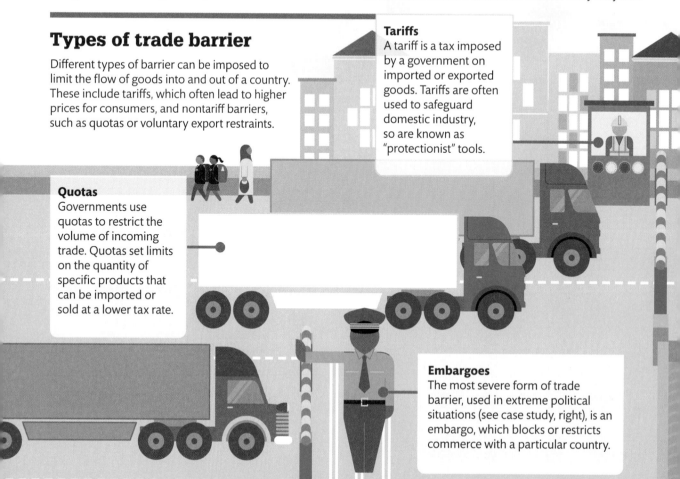

Tariffs
A tariff is a tax imposed by a government on imported or exported goods. Tariffs are often used to safeguard domestic industry, so are known as "protectionist" tools.

Quotas
Governments use quotas to restrict the volume of incoming trade. Quotas set limits on the quantity of specific products that can be imported or sold at a lower tax rate.

Embargoes
The most severe form of trade barrier, used in extreme political situations (see case study, right), is an embargo, which blocks or restricts commerce with a particular country.

be unable to provide the subsidies needed to allow domestic industries to grow and compete in a global market.

While most economists favor free trade over protectionist policies, trade barriers remain a useful political tool. A government that supports domestic industry, reduces unemployment, and maintains quality standards tends to win political favor, as does one that takes a tough stance on unfair competition or imposes economic sanctions on a country in response to human rights abuses or a perceived threat to international peace.

CASE STUDY

Cuba and the United States trade embargo

In 1962, the US placed a full embargo on trade with Cuba in response to the communist takeover led by Fidel Castro. The embargo, which will remain in place until Cuba meets the required standards of democracy and human rights, blocks almost all trade with the country. Tourist travel is banned, but US citizens can now go to Cuba for limited reasons, such as visiting family.

Subsidies
Sometimes governments offer subsidies (financial aid) to domestic industries, such as farming or energy producers, helping them become more competitive and develop new technologies.

Local content requirements
Another type of barrier that favors domestic industry, local content requirements mean that firms must use locally manufactured or supplied goods or services.

Voluntary export restraints
Also called "export visas," voluntary export restraints are agreed between nations, limiting the quantity of some exports to deter the importing state from imposing trade barriers.

Trade and colonization

The discovery of new Atlantic and Asian trade routes in the 15th century opened up the world to Europe. This led to an era of colonial expansion, the effects of which are still felt in many countries today.

From colonization to independence

Between 1500 and 1900, several European nations colonized many regions across the rest of the world. The Spanish and the Portuguese divided South America between them, while the British and the French fought each other for control of North America. India became the most valuable colony of the British Empire, and Africa became a patchwork of countries ruled by various European powers. At the same time, millions of enslaved people from Africa were transported to the Americas, where they were used as labor to cultivate lucrative crops, such as cotton, tobacco, rice, and sugar.

Although most of Europe's colonies are now independent, many of them still bear the scars of colonial rule. Some have descended into civil war, often because their borders were drawn up by Europeans who had no interest in the boundaries that once existed between ethnic groups. Many of these groups became stateless and have since found themselves marginalized by the regimes that came to power when the colonies became independent. Centuries of foreign interference have also left many of these countries lagging behind technologically and dependent on foreign aid.

Reinvested wealth
Colonialism enabled European powers to invest even more in industry and technology, which in turn aided their ability to dominate global trade.

COLONIZER

DECOLONIZATION

The modern period of European colonialism came to an end after World War II. This was mainly because the war had been expensive, and the European powers could no longer afford to maintain their overseas territories. However, it was also due to the fact that the Europeans had enlisted Indigenous people in their respective empires to fight for "freedom and democracy" against Nazi Germany and Imperial Japan, which in turn exposed the hypocrisy of the colonial system.

Mercantilism

The opposite of free trade, mercantilism was an economic system that dominated European trade during the colonial period. States sought to increase their influence at the expense of rival powers by imposing high tariffs on goods from other countries, forbidding colonies from trading with other nations, designating particular ports as marketplaces for particular goods, limiting wages, and maximizing the use of domestic resources.

Cheap raw materials

European nations colonized other countries to control their natural resources, importing raw materials to the mother country to produce manufactured goods.

RAW MATERIALS

MANUFACTURED GOODS

COLONY A

Restricted trade

Colonies were often prohibited from trading for themselves. For example, English trade could only be conducted on English ships, and certain goods could only be shipped to Europe directly.

Colonized people

Colonies provided a supply of cheap, and often, enslaved, labor. Their populations became workforces dependent on their colonizers.

RAW MATERIALS

MANUFACTURED GOODS

COLONY B

Expensive manufactured goods

Colonies served as markets for exported goods. They also increasingly relied on Europe to provide them with sophisticated technologies.

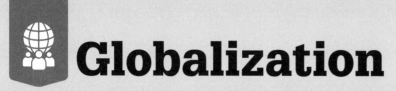

Globalization

The term *globalization* refers to the growing interconnectedness and integration of the world's economies, cultures, and people. The process has been accelerated by technological advances and increased trade.

Network of nations

Globalization includes an increase in trade, investment, finance, movement of people, and flow of technology between nations. This has been fueled by technological advances in communications, particularly the rise of the Internet, and political decisions to remove barriers to global trade and finance. Globalization is linked to the rise of multinational corporations that control the production of goods and services in different countries.

While globalization typically refers to changes during the latter half of the 20th century, there have been earlier phases of globalization. The period between 1600 and 1800 saw increasing trade and cultural exchange with the emergence

Technology

Advances in information and communications technology (ICT), including the Internet, mean that data can now be transmitted instantly around the world.

Political power

The rise in global politics has seen governments unite to tackle international issues. Some argue that globalization has led to the decline in the importance of the nation-state.

Economics and trade

The rapid growth in international trade has led to a greater number of global financial transfers, investments, and multinational companies.

Environment

The increase in consumption, production, and global trade has placed major stresses on the environment and contributed to the climate crisis.

of European empires and the establishment of multinational corporations, such as the British East India Company. This initial phase of globalization was closely linked to the spread of capitalism around the world. In the last 200 years, capitalism—and in particular the rise of neoliberalism—has seen Western countries remove barriers to trade, finance, and investment.

Progress or problem?

Supporters of globalization believe it has led to unprecedented levels of economic growth and produced technological advances that have helped lift millions of people out of poverty and given increased access to technology globally. They highlight the increased cultural exchanges that globalization has brought about—for example, with food, sports, and music.

However, critics of globalization believe that it has, in fact, caused huge increases in inequality around the world, with much of the wealth going to a narrow international elite, leaving millions of people worse off economically. In addition, detractors suggest that globalization erodes national sovereignty and democracy and brings about enormous environmental costs by putting unsustainable pressure on the use of natural resources around the world.

 CASE STUDY

Starbucks

The global coffee chain Starbucks started as a single coffee shop in the American city of Seattle in 1971. After achieving considerable domestic success in the following years, the company sought global expansion and opened its first non–North American café in 1996. Starbucks adopted an aggressive expansion strategy of saturating local markets, with existing local cafés often unable to compete. By 2019, there were more than 30,000 outlets in 80 countries. Starbucks's expansion has had a significant cultural impact, creating a coffee-shop culture in places where coffee was not previously popular.

Community

The growing interaction among people around the world has reinforced the idea of a global community, but some argue that this is at the expense of local communities.

$**19**tn
worth of goods were traded globally in 2019.

United Nations Conference on Trade and Development report (2020)

Culture

The transmission of ideas and values has been driven by the movement of people and technological changes—including social media and streaming services.

An interdependent world

The processes of globalization have meant that what happens in one part of the world increasingly affects others, making the world more interdependent. This mutual dependence affects the global economy as well as various aspects of society. These are often described as different forms of globalization and include technology, trade, politics, culture, community, and the environment.

War and peace

Throughout history, nations have gone to war for a variety of reasons, such as to secure new resources for themselves, to regain territories lost in previous conflicts, or to defend themselves against aggressors. Wars can also erupt within states, either between the government and opposition groups or between regions in conflict with one another. During these struggles, politicians and diplomats may work to establish peace between the warring parties.

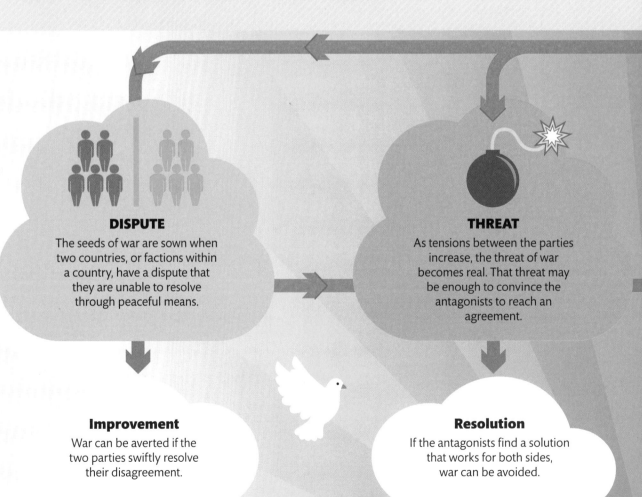

DISPUTE
The seeds of war are sown when two countries, or factions within a country, have a dispute that they are unable to resolve through peaceful means.

THREAT
As tensions between the parties increase, the threat of war becomes real. That threat may be enough to convince the antagonists to reach an agreement.

Improvement
War can be averted if the two parties swiftly resolve their disagreement.

Resolution
If the antagonists find a solution that works for both sides, war can be avoided.

"War **is** an ugly thing, but not the ugliest of things. [The] patriotic feeling **which thinks** that nothing is worth war **is** much worse."

John Stuart Mill, British philosopher and politician, *The Contest in America* (1862)

TYPES OF WAR

Interstate wars

Wars between states, such as the Franco–Prussian War (1870–1871) and the Iran–Iraq War (1980–1988), involve large armies and often begin with one nation invading another. They attract the most international attention because the antagonists are recognized states and often allied with other countries.

Intrastate wars

Conflicts within states, known as intrastate or civil wars, often start as disputes between the government in power and a region or faction that views the government as illegitimate or oppressive. In many cases, such as the Spanish Civil War (1936–1939), both sides are armed or funded by other nations.

UNDERLYING TENSIONS REAPPEAR

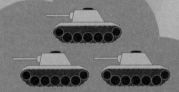

WAR

If the rival parties fail to resolve their dispute peacefully, war becomes inevitable. One side may attack the other, which may then retaliate in kind.

FRAGILE PEACE

After a ceasefire (a break from fighting), the antagonists may agree to peace. However, if their underlying dispute is not resolved, they may soon resume the conflict.

The cycle of war

In many regions of the world, wars flare up repeatedly between the same antagonists, despite the efforts of peacemakers to resolve each crisis. This cycle has a predictable pattern and is generated by the failure of both sides to agree on a solution to the dispute. If the war is over territory or the sovereignty of a nation, the solution often seems impossible, and the conflict only intensifies as casualties increase on both sides.

Permanent peace

The opponents can break the cycle of war if they permanently resolve their dispute.

The right to war

"Just-war theory" is a branch of ethics that examines the questions of when a nation is justified in going to war and how military forces should behave during such conflicts.

Justifying armed conflict

The question of how nations can justifiably go to war was raised across the ancient world by thinkers in Egypt, Greece, Rome, India, and China. However, it was the Christian philosopher St. Augustine of Hippo (354–430 CE) who first used the phrase "just war" and fellow Christian St. Thomas Aquinas (1225–1274) who defined it in the way it is understood today. Aquinas argued that a war is justified when it is commanded by the rightful sovereign, when it is waged for a just cause (such as to repel an invasion), and when the warriors are motivated to do good rather than evil.

He also argued that not waging war could not be justified when doing so would end injustice. Legal theorists such as Hugo Grotius (1583–1645) and Luigi Taparelli (1793–1862) developed Aquinas's ideas and were instrumental in turning them into a set of internationally recognized principles.

By the 20th century, these principles had become international law and were first applied at the Hague Peace Conferences of 1899 and 1907. Later, they underpinned the Geneva Conventions of 1949 and the UN's Convention Relating to the Status of Refugees in 1951. However, international law only applies to

The ethics of war

Traditionally, just-war theorists argued that there are two criteria that can be used to justify going to war. The first is *jus ad bellum* (justice before war), which establishes that the reasons for going to war are just. The second is *jus in bello* (justice during war), which establishes that the war is fought justly and with due regard to avoiding civilian casualties. However, more recently, theorists have added a third criterion, *jus post bellum* (justice after war). This establishes that defeated enemies are treated humanely, are given fair trials, and are not punished disproportionately.

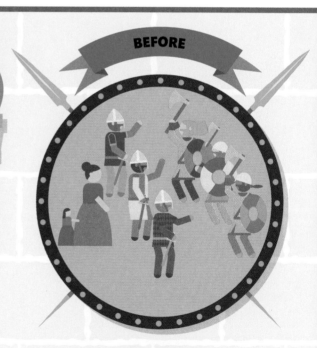

BEFORE

Jus ad bellum

War is justified if it corrects a great injustice, is a last resort, and does not inflict an even greater injustice on the enemy. It must be proportionate, have a high probability of success, and be commanded by a legitimate authority.

"We do not seek peace in order to be at war, but we go to war that we may have peace."

St. Augustine of Hippo, letter to Bonifacium, quoted in St. Thomas Aquinas's *Summa Theologica* (c.1265–1273)

recognized sovereign states and so can only be enforced when combatants represent such states and their decisions. For this reason, the international community is under increasing pressure to rethink international law so that it applies to other kinds of conflict. These include civil wars, which not only are wars within states but are often funded by other states that are involved only to further their own interests.

Establishing peace

Another issue raised by just-war theorists concerns how a victorious nation should treat a defeated enemy nation. For example, many historians have argued that the rise of Nazism in Germany was encouraged by the punitive reparations imposed on the nation after World War I—and that the way in which a war is ended can have a bearing on the next one (see pp.46–47).

THE RED CROSS

The International Committee of the Red Cross (ICRC) was founded by Swiss humanitarian Henri Dunant in 1863, four years after the Battle of Solferino, in which more than 40,000 soldiers were killed or wounded. Originally named the International Committee for Relief to the Wounded, the ICRC was the first organization to help mobilize medical support for soldiers internationally and to ensure that soldiers were given legal protection after battle. Its mission has since expanded to include organizing protection for civilians, mediating between warring parties, treating prisoners of war, and negotiating with detaining authorities. ICRC volunteers wear a white armband bearing a red cross—a symbol that grants them protection under international law. The ICRC is part of the International Red Cross and Red Crescent Movement.

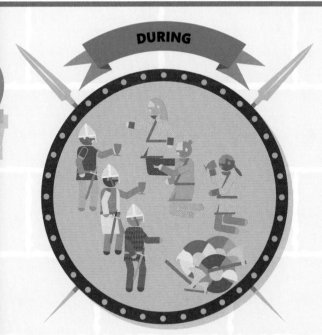

DURING

Jus in bello

During the war, violence should be proportionate, should only be used against enemy combatants, and should only be used to gain a clear military advantage. Harm to civilians should be minimized, and prisoners of war should be treated humanely.

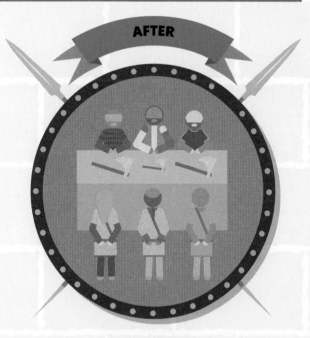

AFTER

Jus post bellum

When a war ends, the victors should publicly declare their victory and agree to peace terms with a legitimate enemy authority. They should not seek revenge and should give fair trials to enemy leaders and combatants.

Alliances and neutrality

In international relations, an alliance is a formal agreement between two or more countries for mutual support in case of war. A neutral state does not support or help either, or any, side in a conflict.

Strength in numbers

States form alliances to strengthen themselves in the face of threats or to boost their power. Alliances have been a feature of global politics since ancient times. The *Arthashastra*, a 4th-century BCE Sanskrit text on statecraft, advises that countries should seek alliances with distant states against neighboring ones — a sentiment expressed in the equally ancient proverb "the enemy of my enemy is my friend." The conflict that consumed Europe from 1914 to 1918 involved so many nations formed into two opposing alliances (the Allies and the Central Powers) that it became the first "world war." Following World War II (1939–1945), some former combatants created new

Alliances and coalitions

In the event of an attack on a nation in an alliance, other members of that alliance are obligated to come to its defense. In this sense, alliances exist to act in a crisis that has not yet occurred. This differs from coalitions, which are formed for a specific military action and are dissolved afterward.

Main combatants

Two countries engage in hostilities. One may have acted as the aggressor against the other, but the end result is armed conflict between their armies.

Allies

Both countries involved in the conflict belong to differing military alliances or coalitions, and those partner countries take sides and join the hostilities.

Cold War alliances in the form of the North Atlantic Treaty Organization (NATO), which combined the US and numerous Western European countries, and the Soviet Union–led Warsaw Pact.

Staying neutral

Some states prefer to avoid alliances, on the grounds that these may draw them into conflicts. Such states may choose to remain neutral, abstaining from participation in wars between other states and remaining impartial toward all combatants. A prime example is Switzerland, which, since its neutrality was established in 1815, has not fought in a foreign war—a way of ensuring external security and promoting peace. It does, however, maintain a standing army in case of attack. Costa Rica, on the other hand, established its neutrality in 1948 by abolishing its military.

Modern conflicts rarely involve legally recognized combatants. More frequently, they are less easily defined conflicts, such as the so-called US War on Terror against extremist groups following the September 11 attacks. Wars of the future will likely take new forms, such as cyber warfare, and traditional understandings of alliances will also need to shift.

> "We have no eternal allies, and we have no perpetual enemies."
>
> Lord Palmerston, former British prime minister, in a House of Commons speech (1848)

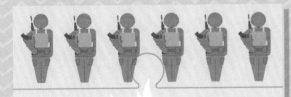

Neutrals

There may be countries neighboring those involved in the conflict that abstain from choosing sides and decide to remain neutral.

TYPES OF NEUTRALITY

Hersch Lauterpacht (1897–1960), an important scholar of international law, identified several types of neutrality.

❯ **Perpetual neutrality** is where the status of a state is permanently neutral by special treaty. Examples include Austria, Malta, Switzerland, and Turkmenistan.

❯ **General and partial neutrality** is where only a part of a state's territory is neutral—for example, by treaty. This happened when the 1864 Treaty of London recognized the Greek island of Corfu as "perpetually neutral"—although that neutrality was subsequently violated on several occasions.

❯ **Voluntary and conventional neutrality** differ in that a neutral status is in some cases purely voluntary, while in other cases a state may be bound by treaty to remain neutral.

❯ **Armed neutrality** is where a state maintains an army in order to protect itself if attacked. This is the case with Serbia and Switzerland.

❯ **Qualified neutrality** allows a state to give some kind of aid to one belligerent. For example, Japan is a neutral country, but it hosts US military bases.

Terrorism

Terrorism is defined as the unlawful use of violence to achieve political ends, whether against civilians during war or in peacetime. It is a term that was first used during the French Revolution of 1789–1799.

Political violence

The words *terrorism* and *terrorist* became widely used in the 1970s, chiefly in relation to acts of violence committed during the Northern Ireland, Basque, and Israeli–Palestinian conflicts. Since then, the words have become associated with suicide bombings and large-scale, indiscriminate acts of violence, such as the November 2008 attacks across Mumbai in India, in which 172 people were killed.

What all of these actions have in common is that they were not perpetrated by soldiers against other soldiers on a conventional battlefield. Instead, they were performed by nonmilitary groups or individuals who specifically targeted civilians at a time when the perpetrators and the target state were not formally at war. However, terrorists may call themselves soldiers and cite the peacetime conditions under which they live as being a permanent declaration of war

Terrorist targets

Terrorist attacks are intended to intimidate a population or to compel a government to pursue or refrain from a certain policy or course of action. They may target specific individuals, random groups of people, or infrastructure, such as gas pipelines or communications networks.

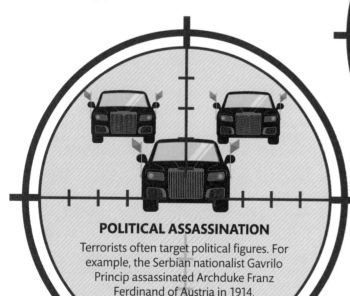

CIVILIANS

Civilians are frequently the victims in terrorist attacks. For example, Islamic militants bombed Madrid, Spain, in 2004, killing 193 civilians and injuring around 2,000 others.

POLITICAL ASSASSINATION

Terrorists often target political figures. For example, the Serbian nationalist Gavrilo Princip assassinated Archduke Franz Ferdinand of Austria in 1914.

"... through education we can fight terrorism... not through weapons."

Malala Yousafzai, Nobel Peace Prize winner (2014)

on the part of their enemies. For example, when Osama bin Laden, co-founder of the Pan-Islamic militant organization al-Qaeda, declared war against the US in 1998, he did so to avenge what he referred to as a century of humiliation that the Arab world had suffered at the hands of the West. He also claimed that killing civilians was justified because, in democracies, civilians are responsible for the actions of the governments they vote for.

Such arguments have been used by many terrorist groups, who often accuse their enemies of perpetrating "state terrorism." Eventually, terrorists may even provoke an enemy into war, such as when a US-led coalition invaded Afghanistan in 2001 in response to the World Trade Center attacks.

THE FAILURES OF TERRORISM

After studying hundreds of contemporary terrorist groups, Professor Audrey Kurth Cronin of American University concluded that terrorism as a political tactic does not work. In a 2011 report, she noted that no terrorist organization has ever been able to take control of a state and that 94 percent of them have failed to achieve even one of their goals.

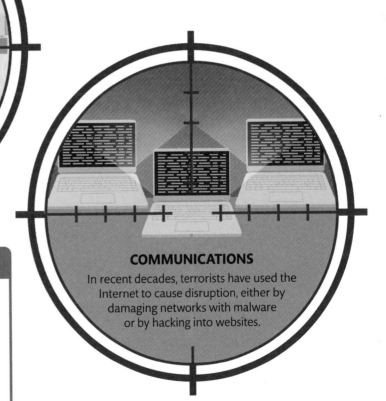

INFRASTRUCTURE

In 2020, the Arab Gas Pipeline was blown up in Syria, causing a blackout across the country. The explosion was attributed to an anti-government terrorist group.

FREEDOM FIGHTERS

Whether a group is considered to be a terrorist organization or not often changes over time. For example, the Kenya Land and Freedom Army, also known as Mau Mau, resisted British rule in Kenya from the late 1940s to the early 1960s. During the conflict, they were considered to be terrorists by the British. However, they have since become widely recognized as freedom fighters who paved the way for Kenyan independence in 1963.

COMMUNICATIONS

In recent decades, terrorists have used the Internet to cause disruption, either by damaging networks with malware or by hacking into websites.

Global concerns

There are many pressing issues that affect the entire world and therefore cannot be solved by individual countries. These issues are collectively known as global concerns. Global institutions that have members from around the world, such as the United Nations (UN), are often best positioned to address these problems by setting priorities and putting pressure on governments to agree to a common set of actions.

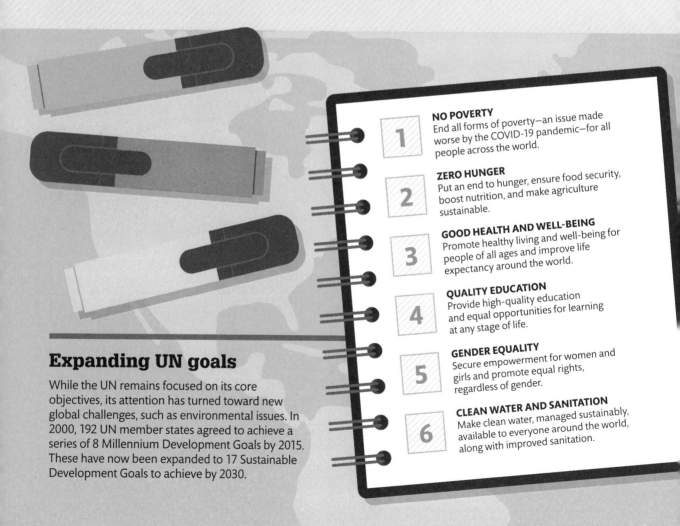

Expanding UN goals

While the UN remains focused on its core objectives, its attention has turned toward new global challenges, such as environmental issues. In 2000, 192 UN member states agreed to achieve a series of 8 Millennium Development Goals by 2015. These have now been expanded to 17 Sustainable Development Goals to achieve by 2030.

1 NO POVERTY
End all forms of poverty—an issue made worse by the COVID-19 pandemic—for all people across the world.

2 ZERO HUNGER
Put an end to hunger, ensure food security, boost nutrition, and make agriculture sustainable.

3 GOOD HEALTH AND WELL-BEING
Promote healthy living and well-being for people of all ages and improve life expectancy around the world.

4 QUALITY EDUCATION
Provide high-quality education and equal opportunities for learning at any stage of life.

5 GENDER EQUALITY
Secure empowerment for women and girls and promote equal rights, regardless of gender.

6 CLEAN WATER AND SANITATION
Make clean water, managed sustainably, available to everyone around the world, along with improved sanitation.

CASE STUDY

The UN and access to COVID-19 vaccines

The UN has co-ordinated the global response to the COVID-19 pandemic from the outset, recognizing that it is not just a health crisis but also an economic one that has highlighted inequalities within and between nations. The WHO outlined public health measures that all countries should implement, with an urgent focus on the poorest nations. As well as providing vaccines for all its personnel, the UN has since lobbied governments to donate vaccines to countries that badly need them.

45%

of the world's children under five receive life-saving vaccines from the UN and its partners.

UNICEF (2021)

 7 AFFORDABLE AND CLEAN ENERGY
Give all people access to safe, sustainable, affordable, and reliable energy sources.

 8 DECENT WORK AND ECONOMIC GROWTH
Aim for long-term economic growth and ensure productive, secure, good, and inclusive employment for all.

 9 INDUSTRY, INNOVATION, AND INFRASTRUCTURE
Make infrastructure resilient and improve the sustainability of industry.

 10 REDUCED INEQUALITIES
Reduce income inequalities within and between countries and help people who have become refugees.

 11 SUSTAINABLE CITIES AND COMMUNITIES
Make cities and other urban settlements safe and sustainable for all, with streets, open areas, and public transportation.

 12 RESPONSIBLE CONSUMPTION AND PRODUCTION
Boost sustainable food production and consumption.

 13 CLIMATE ACTION
Act fast to tackle climate change and its impacts—on communities, ecosystems, food production, and other sectors.

 14 LIFE BELOW WATER
Preserve the oceans, combat pollution and overfishing, and ensure sustainable use of all marine resources.

15 LIFE ON LAND
Protect ecosystems, restore and manage land and forests, and prevent desertification and further loss of biodiversity.

 16 PEACE, JUSTICE, AND STRONG INSTITUTIONS
Encourage peaceful, inclusive societies; make justice available to all; and build accountable institutions.

 17 PARTNERSHIPS FOR THE GOALS
Ensure sustainable development by encouraging higher-income countries to help lower-income countries.

Migration

Humans have traditionally migrated in search of new resources and opportunities as well as in response to hardships caused by armed conflict, human rights violations, or environmental disasters.

Migration patterns

An immigrant is a person who has left their home to settle in a different country. It is estimated that around 272 million people live outside their countries of birth or citizenship—a number that has been steadily increasing in recent years. These immigrants account for around 3.5 percent of the world's population, and they often move to nearby countries.

Emigration takes two forms: voluntary, which is moving abroad for employment, study, or to reunite with family; and forced, which is leaving to escape persecution, conflict, repression, or natural disasters. Those forced to emigrate, often referred to as refugees, are legally covered by the 1951 UN Refugee Convention. This states that the first country in which they find refuge—once they are formally registered as refugees—is obliged to provide them with assistance and protection for as long as the threat in their home country persists. Refugee crises currently account for the most rapid growth in the number of global immigrants, although the number of refugees has actually declined in recent years.

Impact on host countries

International migration changes the economic, demographic, racial, ethnic, and religious makeup of the host country. As a consequence of this, the arrival of immigrants always has a social impact. Some may perceive this positively, perhaps noting the newcomers' contribution to the economy, the increase in the birth rate, and the greater cultural diversity. Others may view the social impact negatively, as a drain on social services or a cause of community tensions due to segregated populations.

THE SYRIAN REFUGEE CRISIS

The conflict in Syria began in March 2011, when pro-democracy demonstrations were forcibly crushed by government troops. The violence spread nationwide, and Syria quickly descended into civil war. As a result, more than half the country's population (about 13.5 million Syrians) have been forced to leave their homes. Of those displaced, 6.8 million refugees and asylum seekers (immigrants applying for refugee status) have fled to neighboring countries, such as Turkey, Lebanon, Jordan, and Iraq, or further afield to Europe and the US. Those who remain in Syria face a humanitarian crisis.

Causes of migration

While persecution, war, natural disasters, economic pressures, and the desire to join relatives remain some of the main causes of migration, people smuggling and human trafficking (the illegal trade in moving people across borders) are of growing concern. An estimated two million women and children are trafficked globally each year as part of an increasingly organized criminal network.

Persecution

Oppression because of a person's ethnicity, religion, race, politics, or culture can push them to leave their country of origin.

The quicker the immigrant population is able to integrate, by gaining employment, for example, the more likely they are to be viewed as having a positive effect.

International immigrants make significant contributions, not only in their host countries—where they often fill employment gaps and help regenerate regional economies—but also in their countries of origin, since they often send money home to the family members who remain.

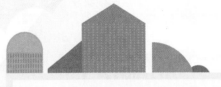

A better future

In recent years, the countries that have accepted the most immigrants include Germany, the US, Turkey, Canada, the UK, Uganda, and Colombia. People travel to these and other countries in search of better prospects.

Natural disasters

Earthquakes, rising sea levels, floods, droughts, extreme desertification, and infectious diseases are likely to contribute to a rise in global migration in the future.

Joining relatives

Joining family is a major reason for migration. The US, for example, grants around 65 percent of permanent visas for family reunification.

War

Conflict has traditionally contributed to the largest spikes in international migration.

Economics

People look for greater economic opportunities, better educational prospects, and an improved standard of living abroad.

Nearly **45%** of US Fortune 500 companies **were** founded by immigrants or the children of immigrants.

The New American Economy Research Fund (2019)

Geopolitics

Geography has always played a major role in shaping the political landscape, particularly the balance of power between nations.

The balance of power

States, empires, and colonial powers have always tried to gain control over territory, populations, and key natural resources in order to guarantee their own survival. Historically, most wars have been fought on that basis, and although aggression is now illegal under international law, geography still plays a crucial role in international politics.

Geopolitical theorists try to understand how the changing nature of the world's resources influences the power of states and the relationships between them. In the past, their goal was to advise states on how to maximize power in a constantly changing environment while also keeping conflict to a minimum. They argued that this could be achieved by maintaining a "balance of power," whereby powerful states aligned themselves in such a way that they balanced each other out. The Cold War was an example of such power balancing.

Land and sea

Many theorists predicted the fall of the early European empires and the rise of new powers, such as Russia, the US, and China, which had control over the largest and most resource-rich territories. They also argued over which factors would determine which states would dominate the modern world. For example,

Competing for control

Geopolitical thinkers predict that the political landscape of the future will be dominated by the US and China. Whether one power is dominant over the other or some kind of power balance is maintained between them, there are various geopolitical issues that may define their relationship.

Cheap labor
Many countries, particularly in the Indian subcontinent and Southeast Asia, provide cheap labor to multinational companies, raising concerns about exploitation.

Border control
With migration on the rise, many territories, such as the US and the European Union, are taking increasingly strong measures to secure their borders.

Trade routes
In an increasingly globalized world, with industries relying on foreign goods, the control and maintenance of trade routes are becoming ever more critical.

Brain drain
As many countries seek to give preferential treatment to migrants with key skills, many smaller countries are losing entire sectors of specialists.

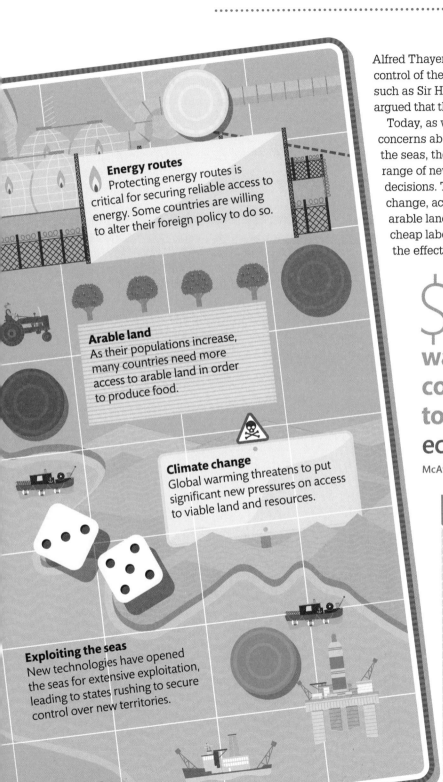

Energy routes
Protecting energy routes is critical for securing reliable access to energy. Some countries are willing to alter their foreign policy to do so.

Arable land
As their populations increase, many countries need more access to arable land in order to produce food.

Climate change
Global warming threatens to put significant new pressures on access to viable land and resources.

Exploiting the seas
New technologies have opened the seas for extensive exploitation, leading to states rushing to secure control over new territories.

Alfred Thayer Mahan (1840–1914) argued that control of the seas was essential, while others, such as Sir Halford Mackinder (1861–1947), argued that the key factor was control of Eurasia. Today, as well as considering traditional concerns about trade routes and who controls the seas, theorists take into account a wide range of new factors that influence state decisions. These include the effects of climate change, access to food, pressures to expand arable land, globalization and the market for cheap labor, big data and cybercrime, and the effects of increased migration.

$6tn
was the predicted cost of cybercrime to the global economy in 2021.
McAfee, security software company (2021)

CASE STUDY

A new Arctic

The Arctic's melting ice is opening up new sea lanes, which could shorten shipping routes by up to half and provide access to new sources of oil and gas. The eight members of the Arctic Council—Canada, Denmark, Finland, Iceland, Norway, Russia, Sweden, and the US—are each eager to maintain control over these routes and resources. To ensure this, they have substantially increased their military presence in the region.

Foreign aid

Historically, countries only gave aid to their military allies or their colonial territories. However, in the modern era, many governments see it as their duty to offer assistance to developing countries.

The origins of foreign aid

Until recent decades, there were two main kinds of foreign aid: military assistance from one strategic ally to another and infrastructure assistance from a colonial power to its colony. However, in the aftermath of World War II, two new factors came into play: the US-sponsored Marshall Plan, which provided aid to 16 European countries that signed up to the initiative, and the founding of new international organizations, such as the United Nations and the World Bank (see pp.164–65). These institutions in particular played a crucial role in determining the allocation of foreign aid in the postwar period. Other major country-led aid programs started off as initiatives to manage reparations after World War II (paid in particular by Germany and Japan) and to deliver aid to former colonies after they had gained independence.

Official Development Assistance (ODA)

ODA is the most common type of foreign aid today. Aimed at promoting development and combating poverty, it is usually given in the form of grants, although sometimes as loans, provided by governments, international organizations, or NGOs. The largest aid givers are the members of the Organization for Economic Co-operation and

Delivering foreign aid

Foreign aid has had a significant impact around the world. Since 1990, it has helped raise many countries out of extreme poverty, cut maternal and child mortality rates in half, increased life expectancy from 65 years to over 72 years, and greatly reduced deaths from diseases, such as smallpox, polio, and malaria.

Education
Aid for education remains crucial, particularly after the COVID-19 pandemic, which has disrupted learning for 1.6 billion students.

Agriculture
Agricultural aid helps countries produce food. This reduces poverty and many sources of conflict, which in turn increases global stability.

Water
Clean water is crucial for maintaining basic levels of health and for fighting the spread of disease. Most water-aid funds go to sub-Saharan Africa.

Development (OECD) and its Development Assistance Committee. These represent the countries of Western Europe, the US, Canada, Japan, Australia, New Zealand, Brazil, China, Iceland, India, Turkey, and the United Arab Emirates, among others.

Since the 1970s, the international benchmark for providing foreign aid has been 0.7 percent of a country's gross national income (GNI). However, only a small number of countries—Denmark, Luxembourg, the UK, Norway, and Sweden—has actually met this target. Although the US remains the largest donor, foreign aid makes up only 0.18 percent of its GNI.

"Foreign aid is an investment, not an expense."

Kay Granger, US politician, *HuffPost* (2011)

TYPES OF FOREIGN AID

Foreign aid is delivered by various institutions, ranging from governments to charitable organizations.

> **Bilateral aid** is direct government-to-government assistance.

> **Multilateral aid** is when multiple governments pool resources with organizations, such as the World Bank, the International Monetary Fund, and the UN.

> **Tied aid** is financial aid that the receiving country must spend on goods produced by the lending country.

> **Voluntary aid** is a charitable donation, particularly when countries are facing a humanitarian crisis.

> **Project aid** is assistance in financing a specific project.

> **Military aid** is similar to tied aid but is specific to weapons and military supplies.

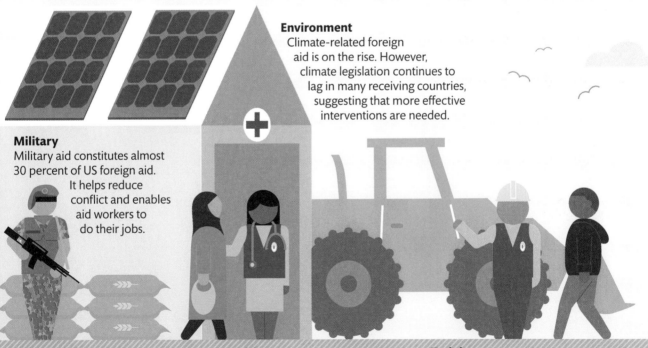

Environment
Climate-related foreign aid is on the rise. However, climate legislation continues to lag in many receiving countries, suggesting that more effective interventions are needed.

Military
Military aid constitutes almost 30 percent of US foreign aid. It helps reduce conflict and enables aid workers to do their jobs.

Humanitarian
Emergency, or humanitarian, aid delivers critical relief to people around the world affected by natural disasters and armed conflict.

Health
Foreign aid for health focuses on the health challenges that affect low-income countries, such as AIDS, malaria, and malnutrition.

Training
Teaching local people to develop new skills, whether as construction workers or as police officers, helps reduce their need for foreign support.

Environmental challenges

Global warming demands that human beings drastically reduce the amount of greenhouse gases, such as carbon dioxide, that they produce. However, enforcing such a change requires strong international leadership.

International agreements

The Paris Agreement was the first legally binding international treaty on climate change. Signed in December 2015 by 196 governments under the UN umbrella, it aimed to prevent the world's average temperature from rising 2°C above pre-industrial levels. However, although the agreement outlined a shared vision and promised financial support for the countries that signed it, it failed to provide a mechanism for enforcing its principles.

Greenhouse gas emissions

In order to lower global temperatures, humanity must reduce the amount of greenhouse gases it produces. This will involve radically rethinking the following key areas of human activity, each of which contributes to global warming.

Electricity
Producing electricity by burning coal, natural gas, or oil accounts for 25 percent of all greenhouse gas emissions.

Buildings
Residential and commercial buildings produce 6 percent of emissions, either by burning fossil fuels for heating or by using toxic products.

Transportation
Gasoline and diesel used in transportation account for 12 percent of all emissions. Aviation, shipping, and trains account for 1.9, 1.7, and 0.4 percent, respectively.

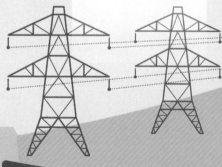

At the same time, the UN set out the Sustainable Development Goals (see pp.184–85) that countries should aim for, although these were not legally binding.

Many environmentalists (see pp.64–65) argue that governments need to take far more drastic action. One such measure is to adjust tax structures and industry incentives in order to increase green innovation and decrease humanity's reliance on highly polluting energy sources. National carbon taxes, for example, have been proven to reduce carbon emissions significantly. However, although around 25 countries have used this tax, few have set it high enough to enforce a significant reduction in greenhouse gas emissions.

FACING THE FACTS

Environmentalists have alerted governments to numerous problems caused by human behavior.

> **Food waste**: A third of the world's food (around 1.3 billion tons) is wasted or lost each year.
> **Biodiversity loss**: Earth's animal population has reduced by more than 68 percent since 1970.
> **Plastic pollution**: More than 11 million tons of plastic go into the oceans annually.

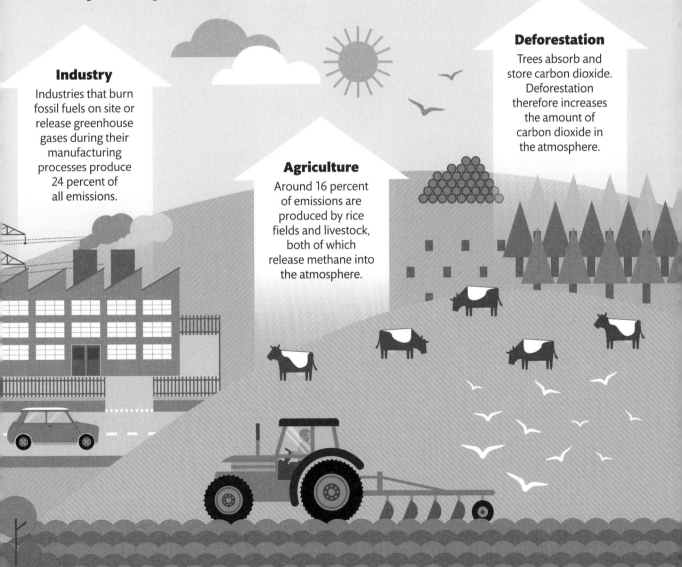

Deforestation
Trees absorb and store carbon dioxide. Deforestation therefore increases the amount of carbon dioxide in the atmosphere.

Industry
Industries that burn fossil fuels on site or release greenhouse gases during their manufacturing processes produce 24 percent of all emissions.

Agriculture
Around 16 percent of emissions are produced by rice fields and livestock, both of which release methane into the atmosphere.

GOVERNMENTS AROUND THE WORLD

This chapter offers an overview of the main governments of the world today. Organized by geographical region, it explores the wide range of political systems that have evolved in recent decades, most of which are rooted in ideas and practices that go back hundreds, if not thousands, of years. Although many political systems are similar, no two governments are exactly the same. Each one has its own philosophy and style of administration, shaped by the unique history and culture of the country it governs.

KEY

 Capital

 Population

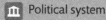 Main languages

🏛 Political system

👤 Head of state

North and Central America

All of these countries practice some form of democratic government and have civil rights enshrined in law. However, violence and corruption in parts of Central America undermine political stability.

Canada

- ⊙ Ottawa
- 👥 38.2 million
- 🗨 English, French
- 🏛 Federal Constitutional Monarchy
- 👑 Monarch of UK, represented by Governor General

Bridging cultures

A federation of former British colonies, made up of 13 provinces and territories, Canada uses the British parliamentary system. The UK monarch is represented by the Governor General, and the prime minister leads government. The lower chamber (House of Commons) is directly elected for five-year terms, while senators in the upper house (Senate) are chosen by the prime minister with no fixed term. Political parties have often built coalitions to bridge different groups and regions, a practice known as "brokerage politics." The province of Quebec is majority French-speaking; a referendum in 1995 rejected independence from Canada by a margin of 1 percent.

INDIGENOUS GROUPS

Since 1982, Canada's constitution has recognized three groups of Indigenous peoples: the First Nations, the Métis Nation, and the Inuit, each with its own culture, language, and history. Despite legal protections, social and economic inequalities exist. The government has begun to address the country's colonial history and its lasting impact; an ongoing process of reconciliation aims to rebuild Canada's relationship with its Indigenous peoples.

Mexico

- ⊙ Mexico City
- 👥 130.8 million
- 🗨 Spanish
- 🏛 Federal Presidential Republic
- 👤 President

Politics under threat

Mexico is blessed with valuable natural resources, but it suffers from significant social and economic inequality and endemic violence. The 1917 constitution guaranteed rights and civil liberties, but in practice, these are impeded by corruption at all levels, organized crime, drug cartels, and regular assassinations of politicians. According to a global report, in 2020, Mexico was also the most dangerous country for journalists to work in.

The president, who is head of state and government, is directly elected for a nonrenewable six-year term. The lower house (Chamber of Deputies) is elected for three-year terms, and the upper house (Senate) for six years. Members can serve two terms, but not consecutively. Voting is compulsory, but this law is unenforced in practice.

Mexico has a diverse Indigenous population, but it is made up of some of the nation's poorest people.

91
politicians were murdered ahead of the 2021 mid-term elections.

www.azcentral.com (2021)

United States of America

- ◉ Washington, D.C.
- ⊟ 333.7 million
- ◉ English
- ⊞ Federal Presidential Republic
- ⊟ President

Starting from scratch

After declaring independence from Britain in 1776, the United Colonies became the United States of America, and the new nation set up its own political system. Rejecting the rule of monarchy, the country's founders formulated a constitution that included checks and balances on power and a Bill of Rights that enshrined personal freedoms.

To balance differently sized states, the 435-seat lower house (House of Representatives) is based on state population; in contrast, every state, no matter its size, is represented by two senators in the upper house (Senate). The president is chosen through a process called the Electoral College (see right). It is possible for a candidate to receive the most votes overall but not win. The 50 states have their own constitutions and governments; tensions can arise over where the boundaries lie between state and federal power.

Low turnouts

US voter engagement is often low. This might partly be due to the difficulties some citizens face in registering to vote in certain states. Recently, concerns about procedure have also been politicized, resulting in a lack of trust in democratic institutions and processes.

Since the days of legalized discrimination based on race, US civil rights have come a long way, but lasting systemic racism still sparks regular political protest.

Electoral College system

In a presidential election, voters cast their ballot. These are tallied, and in 48 states, the winner gets all the electoral votes for that state. Maine and Nebraska assign their electors using a proportional system. A candidate needs 270 votes (out of 538) to win.

Branches of government

By sharing power across three independent branches, the authors of the US Constitution hoped to prevent any monopolization of power.

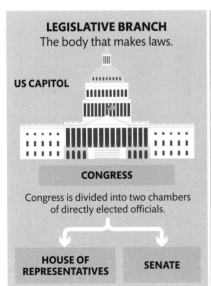

LEGISLATIVE BRANCH
The body that makes laws.

US CAPITOL

CONGRESS

Congress is divided into two chambers of directly elected officials.

→ **HOUSE OF REPRESENTATIVES** → **SENATE**

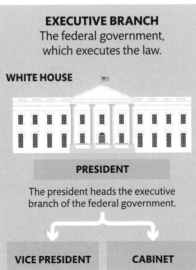

EXECUTIVE BRANCH
The federal government, which executes the law.

WHITE HOUSE

PRESIDENT

The president heads the executive branch of the federal government.

→ **VICE PRESIDENT** → **CABINET**

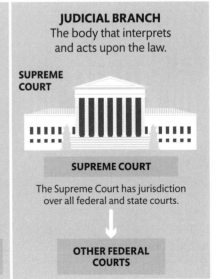

JUDICIAL BRANCH
The body that interprets and acts upon the law.

SUPREME COURT

SUPREME COURT

The Supreme Court has jurisdiction over all federal and state courts.

→ **OTHER FEDERAL COURTS**

Central and South America

In 1979, two-thirds of Latin Americans lived under military rule. Since then, a "third wave" of democratization has swept the continent, but wealth inequality is still an issue.

Costa Rica

- San Jose
- 5.1 million
- Spanish (official)
- Presidential Republic
- President

A model democracy

Formerly governed by Spain and then Mexico, Costa Rica has been independent since 1838. The president (who is head of both state and government), two vice presidents, and 57 deputies in the Legislative Assembly are elected for four-year terms. Politicians can serve two terms but not consecutively, and candidate lists must have equal gender representation. Voting is technically compulsory, but this is not enforced. Election Day is a national holiday, often with a carnival atmosphere.

The judiciary is independent of the executive and the legislature, and the republic has a robust system of constitutional checks and balances. The constitution enshrines equal rights, but in practice, Indigenous minorities continue to face discrimination.

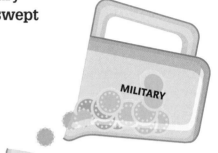

Reallocating military spending
In 1949, Costa Rica replaced its army with a civil guard and invested the savings in other public services.

Venezuela

- Caracas
- 28.3 million
- Spanish, Indigenous languages
- Federal Presidential Republic
- President

A nation in crisis

Venezuela has vast oil reserves, but since 2013, mismanagement by an autocratic regime as well as falling oil prices have led to economic collapse, hyperinflation, and a humanitarian crisis. Millions of citizens have left the country.

Constitutionally, Venezuela is a democratic republic, but the ruling party is authoritarian in practice. In 1998, Hugo Chávez was elected president, and his 1999 constitution added rights for citizens, such as free education and health care.

After the 2019 elections, Juan Guaidó, the opposition leader, declared himself president, an act recognized by around 60 countries. Incumbent president Nicolás Maduro contested the result and remained in office.

17%
of Venezuela's citizens fled the country between 2014 and 2018.

www.worldvision.org (2021)

Brazil

- ⊙ Brasilia
- 👥 214.6 million
- 💬 Portuguese
- 🏛 Federal Presidential Republic
- 👤 President

Coalition presidentialism

Brazil is the world's fifth largest country by area and the sixth most populous. A former Portuguese colony, it achieved independence in 1822 and became a republic in 1889. In the 20th century, military coups punctuated periods of democracy and autocracy, but civilian rule returned in 1985.

Brazil's constitution, rewritten from scratch in 1988, defines it as a democratic federal republic. The president is both head of state and head of government and is elected for a four-year term. The country's unrestricted party system means that it has around 35 political parties, the majority of which are represented in the National Congress. Along with the need to work with federal governors, this creates "coalition presidentialism," in which the president's role falls somewhere between US-style presidentialism and European-style parliamentary coalitions.

Voting is compulsory for citizens between the ages of 18 and 70, unless they are illiterate, in which case it is optional.

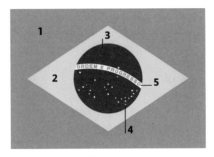

The Brazilian flag
Brazil's flag reflects its history and geography. It has evolved over time and took its current form in 1992.

1. Green is for the land and the color of the first emperor of Brazil's family, the Portuguese House of Bragança.
2. Yellow is for gold and the house of Hapsburg, the family of the first emperor's wife.
3. The blue and white circle replaced the royal arms when Brazil became a republic in 1889.
4. The stars represent Brazil's 26 states and its federal district. They are arranged to correspond to constellations visible in the Southern Hemisphere.
5. Brazil's motto is "Order and Progress."

Chile

- ⊙ Santiago
- 👥 19.3 million
- 💬 Spanish
- 🏛 Presidential Republic
- 👤 President

A revised constitution

After the violent and repressive military dictatorship of Augusto Pinochet from 1973 to 1990, Chile returned to multi-party democracy. In 2019, waves of civil unrest over the increased cost of living led to a plan to write a new constitution. A Citizens' Assembly was elected in 2021. Once it completes the work of drafting and approving a new constitution for Chile, it will be ratified by the country's citizens through a referendum. The current constitution dates from Pinochet's regime and does not recognize Chile's Indigenous people, who make up more than 12 percent of the population.

The directly elected president is head of state and government. Legislative power is shared between the government and the two chambers of the National Congress (Congreso Nacional): the 155-member lower house (Cámara de Diputados) and the 50-seat upper house (Senado). Chile's judiciary is independent, with a Supreme Court as final arbiter.

- ● 28 Left-wing coalition
- ● 25 Center-left coalition
- ● 17 Indigenous groups
- ● 48 Independents
- ● 37 Center-right coalition

Citizens' Assembly
Chile's new constitution will be the first ever created by an equal number of men and women. Seven delegates also publicly identify as LGBTQ+.

Europe

Europe has both republics and monarchies, although all are governed by democratic institutions. Former Soviet states in Europe have redefined their political systems since the fall of the Communist bloc in 1989.

United Kingdom

- ◉ London
- 👤 67.9 million
- 💬 English
- 🏛 Constitutional Monarchy
- 👤 Monarch

Change over time

The UK's system of constitutional monarchy, based on the rule of law and supremacy of parliament, was created over many centuries as power shifted in stages from an absolute monarchy to a representative democracy. The UK's constitution is not a written document of deliberate design but rather a combination of case law, statutes, and conventions developed over time. There is no strict separation of powers: the government (the prime minister and the cabinet) is drawn from parliament. The House of Commons can dissolve government or trigger an election if it passes a motion of no confidence. The UK's blueprint for parliamentary democracy spread to much of the British Empire. In 2020, the UK withdrew its membership in the European Union.

Devolution

Some areas of the UK have devolved powers for making laws and providing public services in areas such as health and education. Northern Ireland has a troubled history, caught between those supporting a united Ireland and those wanting to remain with Britain. Following peace talks, the Good Friday Agreement in 1998 created the Northern Ireland Assembly. Referendums in 1997 saw the creation of parliaments for Wales (which had joined with England in 1536) and Scotland (which had joined the Union in 1707); Scottish independence remains a live issue.

FOUR KINGDOMS

SCOTLAND
NORTHERN IRELAND
ENGLAND
WALES

- ● **Scottish Parliament** 129 members. The first minister leads government.
- ● **Northern Ireland Assembly** 90 members. A system of power sharing means nationalists and unionists must both be represented in the executive.
- ● **Senedd Cymru (Welsh Parliament)** 60 members. The first minister leads government.
- ● **English devolution** 25 directly elected mayors.

UK government structure

The monarch is a ceremonial head of state only. In the lower house (House of Commons), 650 MPs are elected by first-past-the-post voting. The leader of the majority party becomes prime minister and forms a government. Peers in the upper house (the House of Lords) are unelected and serve for life. The judiciaries of England and Wales, Scotland, and Northern Ireland are independent.

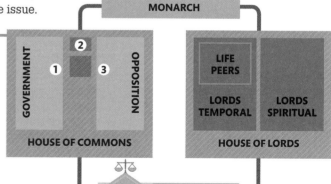

MONARCH

GOVERNMENT | ② ① ③ | OPPOSITION

HOUSE OF COMMONS

LIFE PEERS
LORDS TEMPORAL | LORDS SPIRITUAL

HOUSE OF LORDS

UK COURTS OF LAW

1 Prime Minister **2** Speaker **3** Leader of the Opposition

France

- ⊙ Paris
- 🙂 65.3 million
- 🗨 French
- 🏛 Semi-presidential Constitutional Republic
- 👤 President

Secular republic

France overthrew its monarchy in a revolution that began in 1789. It formed a republic based on the ideals of "liberty, equality, and fraternity." The current system, known as the Fifth Republic, was introduced by Charles de Gaulle in 1958, who replaced a parliamentary republic with a semi-presidential system that split powers between a president as head of state and a prime minister as head of government. If a candidate has no majority in a presidential election, a second ballot is held. The lower house (National Assembly) has 577 elected members, or "deputies"— of which 11 represent France's overseas territories. The upper house (Senate) has 348 members selected by a panel of elected officials. The independent judiciary uses a system of civil law that is based on the principles of the French Revolution. Unusually for Europe, there is a strict separation between Church and state. For example, no religious clothing (such as Christian crosses and Muslim headscarves) can be worn in public institutions, such as schools and government offices.

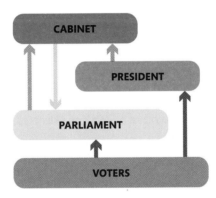

⬆ **ELECTS**

⬆ **FORMS**

⬇ **REMOVED BY**

Premier-presidentialism

In this type of semi-presidentialism, the president appoints the cabinet ministers, but parliament must approve them, and only it can remove them.

Spain

- ⊙ Madrid
- 🙂 46.8 million
- 🗨 Spanish (Castilian), Catalan, Valencian, Gallego (Galician), Euskera (Basque)
- 🏛 Constitutional Monarchy
- 👤 Monarch

A patchwork of nations

After four decades under the dictator Francisco Franco, Spain transitioned to a parliamentary democracy in 1978. The monarch is a ceremonial head of state, and the prime minister heads the national government.

Parliament (Cortes Generales) has two chambers: the lower house (Congreso de los Diputados), with 350 directly elected deputies, and the 265-seat upper house (Senado). Most senators are elected, but some are appointed by regional legislatures.

Spain is a decentralized country of nations rather than a federation. Seventeen autonomous communities and two cities on the North African coast have Statutes of Autonomy and their own legislative and executive branches. The Basque Country, Catalonia, and Galicia also have extra powers. Galicia has nationalist groups, and Basque nationalist parties are popular, but the violent wing of Basque separatism, ETA, disbanded in 2018.

Catalan separatism

In 2017, the Catalan parliament declared independence following a referendum that was ruled illegal by Spain's Constitutional Court. Spain's central government temporarily took control of Catalan institutions.

Germany

- ⊙ Berlin
- 👤 83.9 million
- 🗣 German
- 🏛 Federal Parliamentary Republic
- 👤 President

Global leader

Germany is a parliamentary democracy comprising 16 states. Split into East and West Germany after World War II, it was reunified in 1990 and has since become the world's fourth-biggest economy. Despite having a strong global voice, internal inequalities persist.

Consensus building

Germany's system was designed in 1949 with the aim of ensuring both stability and fairness. In the wake of the Nazi dictatorship in the 1930s, its constitution sought to limit extremist parties. Under the current system, one party rarely obtains enough legislative seats to form a government, so coalitions, negotiation, and compromise are the norm. German governments are often named to reflect the colors of their parties, such as the "traffic light" and the "Jamaica" coalitions.

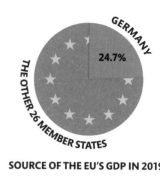

SOURCE OF THE EU'S GDP IN 2019

A dominant force in the EU

Highly industrialized, Germany has a gross domestic product (GDP)—a key measure of economic output—equating to nearly one-quarter of the European Union's total.

Mixed-member proportional (MMP) voting

Voters use MMP to elect the lower house (Bundestag): half the seats are selected directly in 299 constituencies and half by party. Party seats are allocated proportionately to all those over a minimum threshold. There are 598 permanent seats, but the total number varies for fairness. Germany's federal upper house (Bundesrat) has representatives of each state government rather than members who have been directly elected.

Federal structure

The 1949 Constitution outlines five federal organs: the President, the Parliament (Bundestag), the Council (Bundesrat), the Government, and the Constitutional Court.

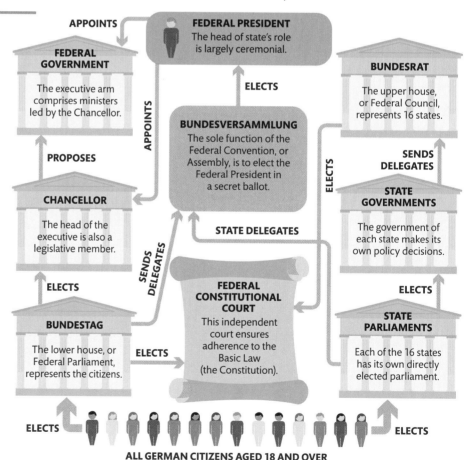

APPOINTS

FEDERAL PRESIDENT
The head of state's role is largely ceremonial.

FEDERAL GOVERNMENT
The executive arm comprises ministers led by the Chancellor.

APPOINTS

ELECTS

BUNDESRAT
The upper house, or Federal Council, represents 16 states.

BUNDESVERSAMMLUNG
The sole function of the Federal Convention, or Assembly, is to elect the Federal President in a secret ballot.

PROPOSES

SENDS DELEGATES

ELECTS

CHANCELLOR
The head of the executive is also a legislative member.

STATE GOVERNMENTS
The government of each state makes its own policy decisions.

STATE DELEGATES

SENDS DELEGATES

ELECTS

FEDERAL CONSTITUTIONAL COURT
This independent court ensures adherence to the Basic Law (the Constitution).

ELECTS

BUNDESTAG
The lower house, or Federal Parliament, represents the citizens.

ELECTS

STATE PARLIAMENTS
Each of the 16 states has its own directly elected parliament.

ELECTS

ELECTS

ALL GERMAN CITIZENS AGED 18 AND OVER

Netherlands

⊙ Amsterdam; Seat of Government: The Hague
👥 17.1 million
🗣 Dutch
🏛 Constitutional Monarchy
👤 Monarch

Global player

The Netherlands is a constitutional monarchy that has developed over centuries, with changing borders, rulers, and politics. Highly industrialized, it has a market economy and a global outlook: it is home to Europol (the EU's law enforcement agency), the International Criminal Court, and the International Court of Justice, and it is a founding member of the EU. The kingdom includes the Netherlands in Western Europe as well as three countries and three municipalities in the Caribbean—a legacy of its empire and influence as a maritime trading nation.

Coalition governing

The power to make laws is shared between the two-house parliament and the executive government—a Council of Ministers led by a prime minister. Tweede Kamer, or the House of Representatives, has 150

members directly elected in a system of proportional representation (PR). Seats in the single constituency are shared respectively among parties, even those with less than 1 percent of the vote. In an election, no party has ever gained an absolute majority, so coalition governments must be negotiated. During this time—the record is 271 days in 2021—the previous government acts as a caretaker "demissionary cabinet." The Senate (Eerste Kamer) has 75 elected members.

Socially progressive

The Netherlands was the first country to legalize same-sex marriage. The 2001 legislation also enabled same-sex couples to adopt children.

Italy

⊙ Rome
👥 60.5 million
🗣 Italian
🏛 Unitary Constitutional Parliamentary Republic
👤 President

Centralized power

Italy has been a republic since abolishing its monarchy by referendum in 1946. In 1948, a constitution was written to safeguard against dictatorship, as had been seen under Benito Mussolini from the 1920s until the end of World War II. A global player, Italy has an advanced economy, although some regional inequalities and reports of corruption and organized crime hamper its progress. Italy is a centralized collection of 20 historically independent and diverse regions, with five having extra powers aimed at preserving their cultural identity.

Political fragmentation

Italy's executive, led by the prime minister, depends on both chambers of the legislative parliament. The lower house (Camera dei Deputati) returns seats in a parallel voting system that includes both first-past-the-post and PR. This benefits minor parties and results in coalition governments. Italy experiences more infighting, allegiance switching, and scandals than other European coalitions, leading to political instability.

69

different governments have held office since 1945.

www.economist.com, "Why does Italy go through so many governments?" (2021)

Norway

- ⊙ Oslo
- 👤 5.4 million
- 💬 Norwegian
- 🏛 Constitutional Monarchy
- 👤 Monarch

Trust and collaboration

Ranked the "best democracy in the world" by the Economic Intelligence Unit, Norway has a good level of public trust and engagement. It has a high standard of living with a low wealth gap, and its society is built on political freedoms and shared values. Party politics tend to be collaborative rather than combative.

Norway's 1814 constitution drew on the British constitutional monarchy, the US constitution, and ideals from Revolutionary France. In 2009, the upper house of parliament was abolished, creating a single legislature (the Stortinget), with 169 members elected by proportional representation. Unlike many legislatures, it cannot be dissolved before the end of its four-year term. The monarch is the ceremonial head of state, and negotiated minority governments are common.

Sámi representation

In 1989, the independent Sámi parliament and administration were set up to represent the Indigenous Sámi people at a national and international level. (Sweden and Finland also have Sámi parliaments.)

ECONOMIC PLANNING
Investment and long-term planning boost the market economy. Norway has a high number of state-owned enterprises.

ORGANIZED LABOR MARKET
The interests of workers and employers are balanced by collective agreements between companies, unions, and the state.

WELFARE STATE
High taxes fund extensive public services, including a generous social security net.

MARKETS

Nordic model

In contrast to the neoliberal approach, Scandinavian countries have social democracies that combine capitalist economics with socialist values.

Poland

- ⊙ Warsaw
- 👤 37.8 million
- 💬 Polish
- 🏛 Unitary Semi-presidential Republic
- 👤 President

Post-socialist democracy

Poland has a strong identity and a long history, despite its borders having fluctuated due to war. After World War II, Poland became a satellite state of the Soviet Union. In 1989, the trade union Solidarity forced the regime to hold elections, returning Poland to parliamentary democracy. Poland's lower house (Sejm), upper house (Senat), and president are all directly elected, and the prime minister leads the government. Poland joined NATO in 1999 and the EU in 2004, but relations have suffered after Poland introduced reforms that restricted the freedom of the media. Within the country, there are also tensions between pro-life Catholic conservatives and people who hold liberal EU values.

1791
was the year Poland adopted its first written constitution.

European Commission, ec.europa.eu (2021)

Hungary

- Budapest
- 9.7 million
- Hungarian
- Unitary Parliamentary Republic
- President

Constitutional changes

In 1989, a new liberal democracy replaced the Soviet-style communist dictatorship that had annulled Hungary's parliamentary system in 1948. The amended constitution, guaranteed by a new Constitutional Court, resulted in a multiparty system, free elections, and a market economy.

Hungary has an indirectly elected president as head of state, but the prime minister heads the executive and wields the most political power, subject to parliament. The legislative National Assembly is elected in a mixed system of direct single-member constituencies and party lists. Hungary joined the EU in 2004, but the EU has raised concerns over constitutional changes and discrimination against the LGBTQ+ community. It is the only EU state to be downgraded to "partly free" by the Freedom House democracy watchdog.

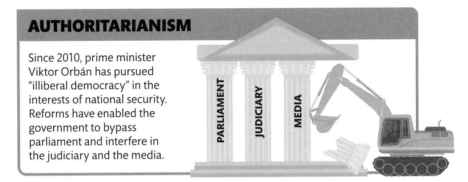

AUTHORITARIANISM

Since 2010, prime minister Viktor Orbán has pursued "illiberal democracy" in the interests of national security. Reforms have enabled the government to bypass parliament and interfere in the judiciary and the media.

PARLIAMENT JUDICIARY MEDIA

Russia

- Moscow
- 145.9 million
- Russian
- President
- Federal Semi-presidential Constitutional Republic

Return to autocracy

After the collapse of the Soviet Union, the political, economic, and social chaos of the 1990s led Russia

Commonwealth of Independent States (CIS)

Russia rules over most of the former Soviet Union with the CIS. Georgia and Ukraine withdrew after Russian military action against them.

to return to its Soviet tradition of having a single strong leader. Since 2000, President Vladimir Putin has brought stability, national pride, and some economic progress, but also authoritarianism. Presidential and parliamentary elections do still take place, but any meaningful opposition has been dismantled, making Russia a one-party state.

MEMBER STATE
ASSOCIATED STATE
FORMER STATE

Africa

Many African nations won independence from colonial rule in the 1950s and '60s. Since then, most have moved from military or single-party rule to multiparty regimes, with varying degrees of success.

Nigeria

- ⊙ Abuja
- 🯅 213.6 million
- 🗨 English (official), Yoruba, Igbo, Hausa
- 🏛 Federal Presidential Republic
- 🯅 President

Developing democracy

Following 33 years of dictatorship, Nigeria embraced democracy in 1999. It became a federal republic, with a new constitution and executive power exercised by the president. However, corruption and election irregularities hamper political and civil freedoms, and recent social media reforms restrict free speech. Security challenges, including radical jihadism and separatist movements, threaten national stability.

Mixed law

The Nigerian legal system is unusual in deriving its laws from four different sources.

ENGLISH LAW
The common law of England, which was adopted during British colonial rule.

COMMON LAW
Laws based on judicial precedent (earlier rulings by judges) since independence.

CUSTOMARY LAW
Laws that incorporate Indigenous norms and practices.

SHARIA LAW
Civil and criminal Islamic law, adopted in 12 northern states since 2000.

Ethiopia

- ⊙ Addis Ababa
- 🯅 119.1 million
- 🗨 Amharic, Oromo, Tigrinya, Somali
- 🏛 Semi-presidential Federal Republic
- 🯅 President

Ethnic tensions

The oldest independent country in Africa, Ethiopia was a monarchy for centuries under the Solomonic Dynasty. Since the 1900s, however, it has experienced a diverse range of political systems, from Marxist-Leninist rule to its current status as a federal democratic republic. It has more than 90 ethnic groups, which has been the cause of political instability, as ethnic tensions have erupted into violence, displacement, and humanitarian crises. In 2020, the Tigray region descended into a full-scale civil war with the state.

The president is head of state and is elected by parliament. The government is led by the prime minister. The lower house is directly elected, and the upper house is elected by state assemblies. However, elections are often marred by arrests, coercion, and registration barriers.

REGIME CHANGES

Ethiopia has experienced turbulent changes of leadership, along with genocide, famine, and civil war.

 1936–1941 Italian occupation, ruled by dictator Benito Mussolini

 1941–1974 Restoration of the monarchy, ruled by Emperor Haile Selassie

 1974–1991 Marxist-Lenin socialist state, ruled by a military junta called the "Derg"

 1991– Federal Democratic Republic

Senegal

- Dakar
- 17.3 million
- French (official), Wolof
- Presidential Republic
- President

Faltering democracy

Since independence from France in 1960, Senegal has been one of Africa's most stable democracies, with relatively liberal civil freedoms. For the first 40 years, there was effectively single-party socialist rule, but in 1999, the incumbent president was defeated by an opposition candidate in an election deemed free and fair by international observers.

The president—the head of state and of government—is directly elected for up to two five-year terms. If no candidate receives more than 50 percent of the vote, there is a second ballot. The single-chamber parliament (National Assembly) is elected for five-year terms using a mixed parallel voting system. Around 96 percent of the nation is Muslim, although there is no official state religion. Political parties compete across ethnic and religious lines.

Although Senegal has a reputation for transparency in government, the executive branch exerts significant control over the judiciary. A report by independent researcher NGO Freedom House states that politically motivated prosecutions of opposition leaders and changes to the electoral laws have reduced the competitiveness of the opposition in recent years.

● **Party Block Vote (PBV)** 90 seats from 45 single and multiseat districts. The party with the most votes receives all of that district's seats.

● **Party Block Vote (PBV) overseas** 15 seats from 10 overseas districts voted for by Senegalese citizens living abroad.

● Proportional representation 60 seats allocated proportionately, according to votes cast for national party lists.

National Assembly
A parallel voting system for Senegal's parliament means that each eligible person has two votes: one Party Block and one proportional representation.

South Africa

- Pretoria, Bloemfontein, Cape Town
- 60.4 million
- 11, including isiZulu, isiXhosa, Afrikaans, English
- Parliamentary Republic
- President

Post-apartheid progress

South Africa's first fully democratic elections were held in 1994. From 1948 to 1991, minority white rule enforced apartheid (a policy of racial segregation in all areas of life), and Black South Africans could not vote. In the new, post-apartheid South Africa, with the majority Black population fully able to participate in national politics, previously banned parties and former political prisoners were elected to high office. Advances have been made in reconciliation and the restoration of rights, but corruption, inequality, and violence continue to limit political progress.

81% of South Africans are Black; 9% are mixed race; 8% are white; and 2% are Asian.

Government of South Africa (2019)

Parliamentary politics

South Africa inherited its parliamentary system from Britain. Citizens elect the lower house (National Assembly), and provincial legislatures elect the upper house (National Council of Provinces). In 2020, the party-list system was ruled unconstitutional because it discriminates against independent candidates: a new mixed system is likely. The president is elected by the National Assembly.

Middle East

Its status as the birthplace of the three major monotheistic religions, along with a legacy of trouble caused by external manipulations, means that politics in the Middle East is complex and often fraught.

Iran

- ⊙ Tehran
- 🚹 85.4 million
- 🗨 Persian (Farsi)
- 🏛 Islamic Republic (Islamic theocracy with elements of Presidential Republic)
- 🚹 Supreme Leader

An Islamic republic

In 1979, revolutionaries overthrew Iran's autocratic and pro-Western monarchy, replacing it with a theocracy. The country has since been ruled by a mix of religious clerics and elected politicians, but it is the clerics who hold ultimate power. Shia Islamic codes are strictly enforced, and civil freedoms are restricted, especially for women and ethnic and religious minorities.

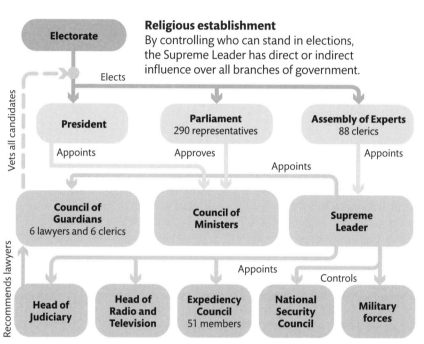

Religious establishment
By controlling who can stand in elections, the Supreme Leader has direct or indirect influence over all branches of government.

Electorate

Elects

Vets all candidates

Recommends lawyers

President

Parliament
290 representatives

Assembly of Experts
88 clerics

Appoints

Approves

Appoints

Appoints

Council of Guardians
6 lawyers and 6 clerics

Council of Ministers

Supreme Leader

Appoints

Controls

Head of Judiciary

Head of Radio and Television

Expediency Council
51 members

National Security Council

Military forces

Saudi Arabia

- ⊙ Riyadh
- 🚹 34.8 million
- 🗨 Arabic
- 🏛 Monarchy
- 🚹 King

The Koran as constitution

Saudi Arabia's constitution is the Koran and the Sunna (Islamic commentaries). The king, who serves for life, selects a male relative as his successor. He is the authority on legislative, executive, and judicial matters, second only to Sharia (Islamic) law. Hundreds of royal princes dominate positions of power. The ulema (religious scholars) are also influential. Restrictions on civil liberties include gender segregation.

Gender inequality

Women are not equal in law and must have a male guardian, which is usually their husband or father.

Without permission from their guardian, women cannot:
- work
- marry
- obtain some health care
- leave prison
- leave a domestic violence shelter

Since 2018, women can:
- drive
- attend public sports events

Since 2019, women can:
- register a divorce, marriage, or death
- register their child's birth
- conduct business on their child's behalf
- obtain a passport
- travel abroad

Turkey

- ⊙ Ankara
- 🯄 83.3 million
- 🗣 Turkish (official), Kurdish
- 🏛 Presidential Republic
- 👤 President

Creeping authoritarianism

Located at the meeting point of Europe, Asia, and the Middle East, Turkey historically bridges the cultures and politics of all three. Once the heart of a great empire, today the country is a democratic republic—even if it is moving steadily toward authoritarianism.

Until 2017, Turkey was a parliamentary republic with a president. A failed coup in 2016 led to a purge of public sector workers, including judges. Prosecutions and

Presidential expansionism
Constitutional reform in 2017 reduced parliamentary oversight and abolished the post of prime minister.

harassment have eroded any real political opposition. Reforms have concentrated President Recep Tayyip Erdoğan's power, and he has deepened his influence over the military, media, civil society,

and religious life. Turkey's secular constitution guarantees freedom of religion, but moves by the increasingly powerful ruling party indicate a shift toward conservative values and a championing of Sunni Islamic causes.

STATELESS KURDS

The Kurds are an ethnic group indigenous to parts of modern-day Armenia, Iran, Iraq, Syria, and Turkey. In Turkey, Kurds make up 15 to 20 percent of the population but have minority status. Turkish authorities class Kurdish rebel group the PKK as a terrorist organization. Kurdish groups have also fought for autonomy in Iraq and Syria.

United Arab Emirates

- ⊙ Abu Dhabi
- 🯄 9.8 million
- 🗣 Arabic
- 🏛 Federation of Absolute Monarchies
- 👤 President

A union of seven

The UAE is a federation of seven independent monarchies, of which Abu Dhabi and Dubai are the most dominant. Though small, the UAE is influential and has abundant oil supplies. The hereditary rulers of each emirate, or state, sit on the Supreme Council, the UAE's highest legislative and executive body. The Council elects the president of the federation from its members, and the president nominates the prime minister.

The Council of Ministers and the Federal National Council (FNC)—a parliament of 40 members with a 50 percent quota for women—are only advisory. Until 2006, all positions were appointed, but today, half of the FNC is elected by a limited electorate. Political parties are banned, and tribal networks are influential. The constitution allows religious freedom, with some qualifications. The judiciary is not independent, and some courts follow Islamic Sharia law.

Eligibility to vote

Most of the UAE's population are foreign workers with no voting rights. The government selects Emirati citizens to vote, but the criteria are unclear.

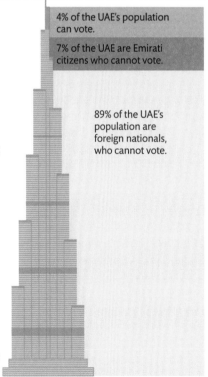

4% of the UAE's population can vote.

7% of the UAE are Emirati citizens who cannot vote.

89% of the UAE's population are foreign nationals, who cannot vote.

Asia

The countries of Asia operate according to a variety of political systems, and the continent is home to most of the surviving socialist states. It has the world's fastest rising economy, though wealth varies.

China

- Beijing
- 1.4 billion
- Mandarin
- Unitary Socialist Republic
- General Secretary of the Chinese Communist Party

Since the 1970s, China has transitioned from a command economy, in which the state dictated production levels and prices, to a market economy that promotes private enterprise— although state-owned enterprises continue to account for more than 60 percent of China's market. Economic growth has rocketed, but often at the cost of employment rights and safeguards.

People's republic

The world's most populous country, China is a nuclear power with a permanent seat on the UN Security Council. Since 1949, it has been a single-party state ruled by the Chinese Communist Party (CCP), in accordance with a mix of Marxist–Leninist communist theory and the philosophy of Mao Zedong (1893–1976), founder of the People's Republic of China (PRC).

China has no opposition parties; dissent is criminalized, and the media is tightly controlled. State Internet censorship and surveillance is so extensive it has been called the "Great Firewall of China." The systematic repression of religious and ethnic minorities in the name of national security in Xinjiang and Tibet has brought China international censure, and Hong Kong has seen increasing political crackdowns.

COMMUNIST PARTY RULE
Executive, legislative, and judicial powers are all held by the Chinese Communist Party. It regulates every aspect of life, including religion, education, and even the number of children that parents may have.

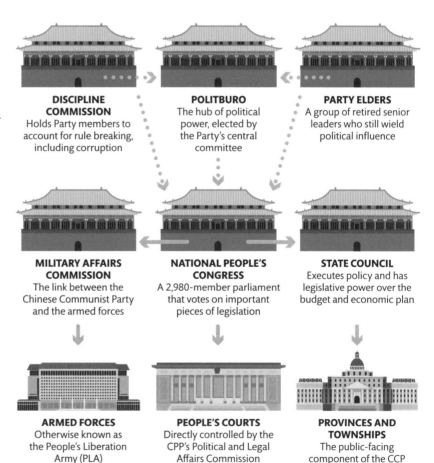

DISCIPLINE COMMISSION
Holds Party members to account for rule breaking, including corruption

POLITBURO
The hub of political power, elected by the Party's central committee

PARTY ELDERS
A group of retired senior leaders who still wield political influence

MILITARY AFFAIRS COMMISSION
The link between the Chinese Communist Party and the armed forces

NATIONAL PEOPLE'S CONGRESS
A 2,980-member parliament that votes on important pieces of legislation

STATE COUNCIL
Executes policy and has legislative power over the budget and economic plan

ARMED FORCES
Otherwise known as the People's Liberation Army (PLA)

PEOPLE'S COURTS
Directly controlled by the CPP's Political and Legal Affairs Commission

PROVINCES AND TOWNSHIPS
The public-facing component of the CCP

APPROVES/ELECTS

INFLUENCES/ADVISES

Japan

- ⊙ Tokyo
- 👤 126.4 million
- 🗨 Japanese
- 🏛 Constitutional Monarchy
- 👤 Emperor

Prosperous archipelago

Although there is still an emperor at the head of the Imperial House of Japan, the role is ceremonial. All the legislative and executive positions are elected, and the judiciary is independent. As one of Asia's oldest democracies, Japan has free and fair elections, civil rights, the rule of law, a free press, and freedom of religious expression.

Legislative power resides with the National Diet—the name for Japan's bicameral legislature—which is composed of two chambers: the House of Representatives and the House of Councillors. The prime minister is appointed from the House of Representatives.

Japan underwent rapid economic expansion after World War II and has since become the third-largest economy in the world. The Japanese constitution, which came into effect in 1947, was largely imposed on the country by the US. It was mostly shaped by American authors and contains many similarities to the US Constitution, particularly in its protection of personal rights and liberties.

AN AGING POPULATION

A high standard of living has resulted in a long life expectancy for the Japanese. But with a declining birth rate, this creates a higher proportion of elderly people, reliant on pensions and health care, compared to the falling number of tax-paying workers.

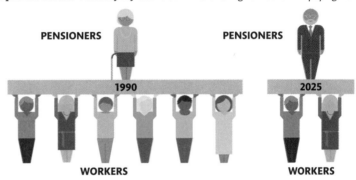

PENSIONERS 1990 WORKERS — PENSIONERS 2025 WORKERS

Singapore

- ⊙ Singapore
- 👤 5.3 million
- 🗨 English, Malay, Mandarin, Tamil
- 🏛 Parliamentary Republic
- 👤 President

Paternalistic state

A former British colony and current member of the Commonwealth of Nations, Singapore has been independent since 1965. Its parliamentary system is based on the British model, although it is not a Western-style liberal democracy. The executive branch is made up of the president and the cabinet. The president's role is largely ceremonial, and it is the prime minister who heads the government. Executive power is exercised by the cabinet, appointed by the president on the advice of the prime minister. The majority party forms the government, and the prime minister is the leader of the majority party. However, in practice, opposition is negligible and the People's Action Party (PAP), a conservative center-right party, has ruled continuously since independence—and the same family, the Lee family, has dominated Singaporean politics since 1959.

Government policy takes a paternalistic approach, with strict rules and regulations. Individual liberties are second to a smooth-running, well-ordered society. The country's rapid economic growth has been credited to government intervention, foreign investment, and migrant workers.

Singapore pays its politicians the highest salaries of any politicians worldwide. It is also rated one of the least corrupt countries globally.

In 2019, the prime minister received an annual salary of

$1.6m.

Government of Singapore (2021)

India

- New Delhi
- 1.39 billion
- Hindi and English (official) plus regional languages
- Federal Parliamentary Republic
- President

Federal republic

India is the world's biggest democracy, a nuclear power, and an emerging economic powerhouse, but it faces inequalities and religious tensions.

Independent from Britain since 1947, India has a parliamentary democracy, with an indirectly elected president replacing the monarch. The 545 members of the lower house (Lok Sabha) are directly elected, with some seats reserved for certain castes and tribes. Most of the 245 seats in the upper house (Rajya Sabha) are elected by regional legislatures. "Semi-federal" India has 28 states and eight union territories, but power is weighted more toward the central government.

With 900 million voters, elections last six weeks. Voting machines are taken around the country: into the Himalayas on yaks, through forests on elephants, and across deserts by camel. Party symbols are used, as one-quarter of Indians are illiterate.

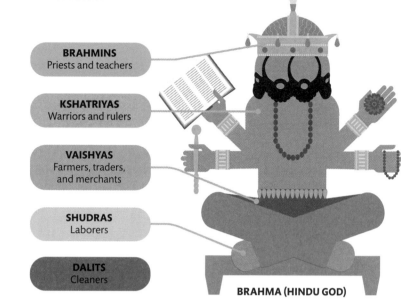

BRAHMINS
Priests and teachers

KSHATRIYAS
Warriors and rulers

VAISHYAS
Farmers, traders, and merchants

SHUDRAS
Laborers

DALITS
Cleaners

BRAHMA (HINDU GOD)

Caste system
In the Hindu caste system, different groups represent the body of the creation god, Brahma. Discrimination based on caste is illegal in India.

Vietnam

- Hanoi
- 98 million
- Vietnamese
- Socialist Republic
- President

One-party system

Vietnam is a single-party state ruled by the Communist Party of Vietnam (CPV), which tightly controls speech, religion, movement, and political activity. Criticism of the government is illegal.

Vietnam's three political structures are the CPV, the government, and the National Assembly, but the CPV holds the most power, including over the judiciary. There are direct elections for the National Assembly, but candidates are vetted before they can stand.

In 1986, the *Doi Moi* economic reform introduced some free-market principles within a socialist framework. Private enterprise was legalized, and foreign investment soared, leading to a transformation in the country's development.

Economic growth
Doi Moi economic liberalization saw a rapid rise in GDP, but the benefits have not reached everyone.

GDP IN US$ BILLION

| 1985 | 1990 | 1995 | 2000 | 2005 | 2010 | 2015 | 2020 |

Thailand

- ⊙ Bangkok
- 👤 70 million
- 🗣 Thai
- 🏛 Constitutional Monarchy
- 👑 King

Military influence

Thailand's absolute monarchy became a constitutional monarchy in 1932. The king has little formal power, but in practice, he holds more influence than European monarchs. Democratically elected governments have been interspersed with military juntas (who have taken power by force). The most recent coup, in 2014, led to a military-drafted constitution that weakened political parties and elected institutions.

Under the current semi-civilian rule, the 500-seat lower house (House of Representatives) is directly elected with a mix of simple majority-vote and party lists. The 250-seat upper house (Senate) is appointed by the military. The prime minister is selected by both houses, giving the army significant control. Pro-democracy protests have been met with crackdowns. Thailand's *lèse-majesté* law makes insulting the monarchy a crime and is considered among the harshest in the world. Judicial independence may be compromised by corruption.

13
successful military coups have occurred since 1932.

www.CNBC.com, "Why does Thailand have so many coups?" (2019)

South Korea

- ⊙ Seoul
- 👤 51.3 million
- 🗣 Korean
- 🏛 Presidential Republic
- 👤 President

Sixth republic

Since its partition from North Korea in 1948, South Korea has become an affluent major economy. Five major revisions to the constitution have led to the Sixth Republic, which began in 1987.

The head of government, the president, is elected every five years and the 300-strong National Assembly every four years using a system known as parallel voting—a mix of proportional representation (PR) and first-past-the-post. In 2019, the allocation of seats gained by PR changed to benefit smaller parties, and the voting age was lowered from 19 to 18. Elections are overseen by the National Election Commission, which has three members selected by the president, three by the National Assembly, and three by the Supreme Court.

A culture of "politics of the person" rather than party loyalty fuels splits and mergers. Corruption and other scandals have added to political volatility. Freedom of expression exists, but some political activity linked to North Korea is banned.

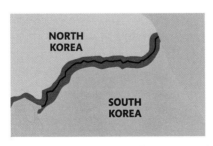

— Military Demarcation Line (MDL)
■ Demilitarized Zone (DMZ)

TWO KOREAS

The percentage of people who use the Internet provides a stark example of the relative prosperity and standard of living between South Koreans and their former compatriots in North Korea—a closed communist state.

NORTH KOREA
<0.1%

SOUTH KOREA
97%

REPORTED PERCENTAGE OF INTERNET USERS IN 2020

Border tensions

The Korean War (1950–1953) never officially ended. A truce line from the 1953 armistice, with a 2.4-mile (4-km) wide buffer zone, is heavily fortified.

Oceania

Oceania is a geographic region that includes Australia, New Zealand, and numerous Pacific island nations, most of which are parliamentary democracies.

New Zealand

- ⊙ Wellington
- 👥 4.9 million
- 🗨 English, Māori
- 🏛 Constitutional Monarchy
- 👤 Monarch, represented by a Governor-General

- ■ GENERAL ELECTORATE SEAT
- ■ PARTY LIST SEATS
- ■ MĀORI SEATS

Parliamentary change

New Zealand has a relatively short political history. The first settlers are thought to have come from Polynesia around the 13th century, and their Māori descendants constitute roughly 16 percent of today's population. Mass European immigration began in the 19th century, under British rule, when a version of "Westminster" politics was established. In 1950, New Zealand dissolved its upper chamber, and in 1993 changed first-past-the-post (FPTP) voting to mixed-member proportional representation (PR). Parallel systems of electoral districts exist in order to ensure Māori representation: a general roll and the Māori roll. Electors only vote in one, but those of Māori descent can choose which to join.

Socially progressive

In 1893, New Zealand became the first country to give women the vote, and in 2017, a river sacred to the Māori, the Whanganui, became the first river in the world to ever be granted the legal rights of a person.

Many progressive laws began as members' bills (bills introduced by MPs who are not government ministers)—for example, marriage equality (2013) and assisted dying (2021). More bills are submitted than there is time to debate them, so numbered counters are drawn from a humble 30-year-old cookie tin to decide which members' bills will be debated.

House of Representatives
After the 2020 election, parliament had 120 seats: a mix of closed party list seats, and individuals elected from the general and Māori rolls.

Commonwealth country

New Zealand's head of state is the British monarch. He or she appoints a Governor-General, on the advice of the New Zealand prime minister, to carry out royal constitutional and ceremonial duties in New Zealand. Like the UK, New Zealand is rare in not having a single constitutional document—instead, it has an amalgamation of written and unwritten sources.

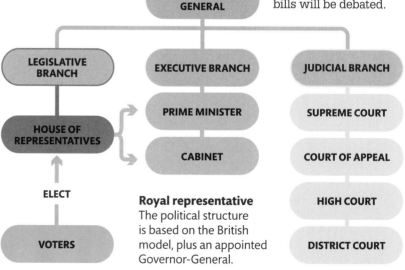

MONARCH

GOVERNOR-GENERAL

LEGISLATIVE BRANCH — EXECUTIVE BRANCH — JUDICIAL BRANCH

HOUSE OF REPRESENTATIVES → PRIME MINISTER — SUPREME COURT

→ CABINET — COURT OF APPEAL

ELECT — HIGH COURT

VOTERS — DISTRICT COURT

Royal representative
The political structure is based on the British model, plus an appointed Governor-General.

Australia

- Canberra
- 25.9 million
- English
- Federal Constitutional Monarchy
- Monarch, represented by a Governor-General

Post-colonial politics

As a former British colony, Australia follows the Westminster model of parliamentary democracy. The government, led by the prime minister, is drawn from the lower house (House of Representatives), as are an official opposition and shadow cabinet of ministers. Both houses of parliament are directly elected every three years. These days, Australia uses a mix of preferential voting and proportional representation, but it previously experimented with many voting systems. The head of state is the British monarch, represented by the Governor-General. Unlike in the UK, voting is compulsory. Constitutional change must be ratified by a referendum.

FEDERATION OF STATES

Australia's six states and two self-governing territories have their own constitutions, laws, and legislative and executive branches. Regardless of the size of their populations, each state returns 12 members to the upper house of the federal parliament (Senate), and each territory sends two. Senators are elected for six years, with half of their number up for reelection every three years.

Indigenous reparations

Aboriginal and Torres Strait Islander peoples had lived in Australia for millenia before Europeans arrived. State crimes against them still reverberate today. It was not until 1967 that Indigenous people were included as part of the population. In 2008, the government formally apologized for past wrongs, and a process of reconciliation is ongoing, although systemic inequality persists.

Three tiers of elections

Australians vote at three levels. Polling stations often have stands selling sausages in bread to raise funds, commonly known as "sausage sizzles."

Local government

Councillors are elected to city or shire councils. Their responsibilities include road repairs, trash collection, and public health.

State or territory parliament

All states but one have two chambers, and the territories have legislative assemblies, looking after local concerns, such as health and education.

Federal parliament

Responsibilities of the elected federal government, drawn from parliament, include foreign affairs, defense, trade, and immigration.

54.9%

voted against Australia changing to a republic in a 1999 referendum.

www.bbc.co.uk (1999)

Index

Page numbers in **bold** refer to main entries.

Acknowledgments

Dorling Kindersley would like to thank Heather Wilcox for Americanization; Debra Wolter for proofreading; Vanessa Bird for the index; Sarah Mahomed Ross, Jonathan Ward, and Philippa Willitts for authenticity reading.